Lesotho and its Governing System.
One Leadership of all time

Author
Shadrack Leabua

SONITTEC PUBLISHING. All rights reserved. No part of this publication may be reproduced, distributed, or transmitted in any form or by any means, including photocopying, recording, or other electronic or mechanical methods, without the prior written permission of the publisher, except in the case of brief quotations embodied in critical reviews and certain other noncommercial uses permitted by copyright law. For permission requests, write to the publisher, addressed "Attention: Permissions Coordinator," at the address below.

Copyright © 2019 Sonittec Publishing
All Rights Reserved

First Printed: 2019.

Publisher:
SONITTEC LTD
College House, 2nd Floor
17 King Edwards Road,
Ruislip
London
HA4 7AE.

Content

Content 5

Lesotho and its Governing System 1

The Topic *1*
    Equal participation in public institutions 2
    Consultation and participation in policy development 4
    The mass media 5
    Elections and electoral process 8
    Political parties 12
    The legislature 16
    Local government structures 19
    Traditional authorities 22
    Development assistance and foreign relations 26
    Conclusion and recommendations 28

Chapter One *33*
    Introduction 33
    Background and context 35
    Conclusion 53

Chapter Two *54*
    Constitutional framework: TheConstitutionand international standards 54
    Development of the Constitution 61
    The dual-citizenship case of Pholoana Adam Lekhoaba 63
    Political participation and gender empowerment/ discrimination 65
    Conclusion and recommendations 67

Chapter Three *69*
    Equalcitizenship 69
    Non-discrimination and affirmative action 71
    Equal participation 74
    Migrants and refugees 75
    Conclusion and recommendations 76

Chapter Four *78*
    Participation in the policy process 78
    Freedom of expression and press freedom 78
    Access to information 85
    Freedom of association 87
    Consultation and participation in policy development 89
    The strength of civil society 92
    Conclusion and recommendations 93

Chapter Five 96
   Elections 96
      A. Legal and institutional framework 96
      Electoral administration 97
      Voter registration, education and participation 101
      Electoral system 104
      Electoral malpractice 105
      Election observation 108
      Validity of results 111
      Conclusion and recommendations 112

Chapter Six 115
   Political parties 115
      Constitutional and legal framework for political parties 115
      Party organisation and membership 123
      Internal democracy and participation in policy development 124
      D. Party funding 126
      The strength of the political party system 130
      Party organisation and membership 142
      Conclusion and recommendations 144

Chapter Seven 146
   The legislature 146
      Legal framework 146
      Attempted vote of no confidence in the government of Lesotho 150
      Membership 152
      Law-making and oversight 157
      Committees 164
      Participation in the work of the legislature 168
      Control and audit of parliamentary finances 171
      Efforts towards strengthening Parliament 172
      Conclusion and recommendations 173

Chapter Eight 176
   Local government 176
      Structure 179
      Access to information 185
      Oversight of local executives 186
      Participatory democracy 187
      Conclusion and recommendations 189

Chapter Nine 190
   Traditional authorities and the institution of chieftainship 190
      Constitutional and legal recognition of traditional leadership 192
      The role of traditional leadership in public life 196
      Systems of accountability of traditional leadership 197

    The debate on the role of traditional leadership 199
    Interaction of the chieftainship with elected national Parliament 201
    Conclusion and recommendations 203

Chapter Ten *204*
    Development assistance and foreign relations 204
    Democratic debate and foreign policy 204
    Access to information 206
    Harmonisation of financial resources 209
    Conditionality 212
    Aid supporting democratic development 213
    Assistance to civil society organisations for engagement with
    government bodies 215
    Conclusion and recommendations 216

Lesotho and its Governing System

The Topic

The Kingdom of Lesotho will be marking 20 years of its return to multi-party politics in 2013 after being ruled by two undemocratic regimes: authoritarian rule under the Basotho National Party (BNP) from 1970 to 1986 and rule under a military junta from 1986 to 1993. From 1993 to date, the country has held five rounds of parliamentary elections (1993, 1998, 2002, 2007 and 2012). The elections have, undoubtedly, granted the citizens of Lesotho an opportunity to participate in the selection of their representatives and rulers. The outcomes of these elections were only accepted by all political parties in two instances, namely the elections of 2002 and 2012. The others were rejected by the losing parties because of the exclusionary effect of the then First-Past-The-Post (FPTP) electoral system bequeathed by Britain to Lesotho at independence.

After the introduction of the Mixed Member Proportional (MMP) electoral system in 2002, however, Lesotho has experienced unprecedented levels of political stability. The country has attained a remarkable and peaceful alternation of power and the establishment of a democratically elected coalition government – a rarity not only in Lesotho, but also on the African continent as a whole. This is undoubtedly a commendable achievement.

Crucial questions that nevertheless remain are:

- Do the Basotho, individually and through their different institutions (political parties, civil society, the media, the legislature, local government structures and traditional leadership) enjoy a broader scope for participation in political and public-policy processes than before?
- To what extent are these institutions working effectively as instruments for political participation?

Equal participation in public institutions

Lesotho is a largely homogeneous society and, over the centuries, intermarital arrangements across different clans have helped to prevent issues of social differentiation based on ethnicity, religion or other features affecting some societies on the African continent. As such, rights to participate in national politics are generally enjoyed by citizens across the nation. The national legislature, the executive and the civil service are broadly representative of almost all geographic regions of the country. No serious issues have been raised by any group about underrepresentation. By way of example, the state provides scholarships for tertiary education, which generally benefit every qualifying student, as well as pensions for all citizens from the age of 70. 1 Women and the youth are largely able to exercise their right to participate in national politics. The government has taken deliberate affirmative-action measures to appoint women to senior positions in the public service. For example, in the post-2007 elections Cabinet, there were nine women (seven Ministers and two Assistant Ministers), who constituted 39% of the overall Cabinet. Following the 2012 elections, five women were appointed as Ministers and three as Deputy Ministers. This means that the Cabinet currently enjoys 27% women representation, which reflects a 12% decline from the previous Cabinet. So far, these affirmative-action policies have not made much impact on national politics. In most instances, women are selected or appointed for public-service positions for a given period, after which they simply return to their previous positions in society. This suggests that there is an urgent need on the part of the government and civil society organisations, especially organisations representing the interests of women, to conduct empirical studies to establish what more should be done not only to defend the gains the country has already made towards gender parity, but also to identify obstacles to the social promotion of women in society.

Consultation and participation in policy development

The public policy-making process in Africa has been the preserve of the political and bureaucratic elites since independence. Nhema captures this issue succinctly when he notes that 'public policies in Africa are very conservative and restricted, with very little public involvement and no input from [the] wider community'. Lesotho is no exception to this practice, even after almost 20 years of plural politics. Civil society in Lesotho has to fight for participation in the formulation of public policies. This can perhaps be explained in terms of a long history of authoritarian rule that was, by nature, extremely secretive. Even currently, civil servants are generally not allowed to release information to the public without authorisation by the respective heads of ministries and chief accounting officers (locally called principal secretaries).

Similarly, citizens do not make any inputs in the preparation of the national budget. This process remains highly elitist. The budget is mainly informed and developed by departments of government. In the past few years, there has been a cosmetic exercise in which different sections of society are invited to selected venues at which the Minister of Finance comments on the budget after it has been presented to Parliament. The value of these meetings is highly suspect, given that they have no effect on any of the proposed budgetary allocations. Government departmental planning schedules are almost non-existent in Lesotho, and, where they exist, such schedules are not open to the general public. One rare case has been the development of the Poverty Reduction Strategy Paper (PRSP) that allowed participation by civil society organisations, including the Lesotho Council of Non-Governmental Organisations (LCN), the Transformation Resource Centre (TRC) and traditional chiefs. However, the implementation of the Millennium Development Goals (MDGs) by government was a closed process which took place without any involvement of civil society at all. Furthermore, implementation of the MDGs is haphazard. Government does not have clearly specified plans reflected in the annual national budget for the achievement of the MDGs, and there is no link between what government and civil society are doing towards achievement of the MDGs.

The mass media

Since the return to multi-party politics in 1993, Lesotho has witnessed a growing number of private media institutions, both print and electronic. This is a positive development, as it provides citizens with avenues for exercising their rights and allows them to participate in national issues. Generally, citizens of Lesotho have been enjoying a high degree of freedom of speech, including criticising their governments freely since the 1993 transition to multi-party politics. Following the historic May 2012 parliamentary elections and the resulting democratically elected coalition government, even Ministers now take part in public debates on phone-in programmes broadcast by private radio stations on key national issues. This is good for the accountability and the responsiveness of public officials.

But serious challenges remain in respect of the state-owned media (Radio Lesotho and Television Lesotho), which are the only media to enjoy national coverage of the country and which remain firmly under government control. The government dictates what should be broadcast and who should have access to these institutions for the purpose of expressing views and disseminating information. Opposition parties only have access to government-owned media at the express will of the government. The only exception is during official election campaign periods when the Independent Electoral Commission

(IEC) allocates almost equal time to all registered political parties for formal party-political broadcasts as provided for under section 67 of the National Assembly Electoral Act, 2011. News coverage of political-campaigning activity, however, remains firmly under the control of government-appointed journalists and editors and is slanted in favour of the ruling parties.

The private media continue to face challenges as well. One of these is that Lesotho still maintains outdated media legislation that substantially hinders media freedom. These include, for example, the Printing and Publications Act, 1967; the Official Secrets Act, 1967; the Sedition and Proclamation Act of 1967; and the Internal Security Act, 1984. Media practitioners and media freedom advocates firmly believe that these laws inhibit the operations of free and independent media, access to information and freedom of expression in the country.

Lesotho does not have a law to facilitate access to government-held information by citizens and the media. The media fraternity has, for over 11 years, been urging the enactment by Parliament of the Access and Receipt of Information Bill, 2000, without any success. Without such information, the media are not able to play an effective watchdog role on behalf of citizens.

The lack of media freedom in the country seriously undermines the principles of transparency and accountability of state institutions.

The Lesotho Parliament has also passed the Public Meetings and Processions Act, 2010. This act makes it mandatory for anyone holding public meetings or processions to first seek and obtain permission from either the police or the chiefs of the areas where such meetings or processions are to be held. The act has caused controversy among civil society organisations because it gives the police and chiefs powers to undermine the right to freedom of association. Before the act was introduced, the Basotho were only required, by the Public Meetings and Processions Act, 1993, to inform the police about the processions and meetings they intended to hold.

Elections and electoral process

Elections are the main institutions providing citizens with a chance, and, indeed, which accord them the right, to participate in the selection of their representatives in modern democracies. The Basotho exercised this right during the 1965 elections. However, since then until the return of Lesotho to multi-party politics in 1993, elections seem to have caused more problems of conflict than they have solved. But having implemented constitutional and electoral reforms from 1997, when the IEC was established, and from 2002, when the MMP system was introduced, Lesotho seems to have found a formula for political stability: an inclusive Parliament, and, most importantly, an elected coalition government. This is arguably the best innovation worthy of emulation in other countries bedevilled by election-related conflict. However, the system also features a number of inherent drawbacks, prominent among which is its operational complexity in translating citizens' votes into parliamentary seats. Its implementation also requires massive voter education to help voters understand how to utilise their ballot/s to achieve their desired outcomes. This is even more essential when the principle of two votes per voter is used, as was the case in the elections of 2002. Overall, however, it appears to be better for voters to cast one ballot only, which is counted both for the determination of Proportional Representation (PR) and FPTP seats, as Lesotho did in the 2012 elections.

In all elections since 1993, the Basotho have voted freely without incidents of violence or intimidation. However, voter turnout has been declining, most probably because, while voter registration is legally compulsory, voting is not. In the first elections, which led to independence in 1965, voter turnout was 62. 32%, and increased significantly to 81. 90% in the following polls of 1970. Between 1970 and 1993, there were no elections, given that the then BNP government took power by force after 1970 and ruled the country until it was toppled by the military in January 1986. The military government organised elections in 1993, which were won overwhelmingly by the Basutoland Congress Party (BCP). In these elections, the voter turnout was 72. 28%, only to decline slightly by 1% to 71. 28% in the 1998 elections. In subsequent elections, the turnout saw a further downward trend from 66. 69% in 2002 to a low of 49. 00% in 2007 and to 50. 04% in the 2012 elections.

There are no studies to explain trends in, or patterns of, voter turnout in Lesotho. As such, the factors causing this downward trend can only be speculated about. The years in which the Basotho went out to vote in relatively large numbers, namely 1970, 1993 and 1998, were unique in the political history of the country. In 1970, voters possibly wanted to remove the BNP from power after being disappointed with its governance performance and to replace it with the BCP. In 1993, too, it could be argued that voters wanted to remove the military junta and replace it with an elected civilian government in keeping with the generally prevailing process of third- wave global democratisation. The 1998 turnout could be explained in terms of the desire on the part of the voters to ensure that the process of democratisation did not suffer reversal or erosion. In subsequent years, voters could have become disillusioned by a virtually one-party-dominant system under the Lesotho Congress for Democracy (LCD).

All elections from 1998 were run by the IEC, a new body established in 1997 to replace the Electoral Office. When it started its work in preparation for the 1998 elections, the Commission was criticised by the opposition for lack of transparency and managing elections in ways that favoured the ruling party. In preparing for the 2012 elections, the Commission probably learnt from its former shortcomings and made itself more open and transparent than in the past. It worked very closely with its stakeholders – the leadership of political parties and civil society. Politicians served on practically all committees of the Commission related to management of the election. The National Assembly Electoral Act, 2011, also provides, under section 122, for a binding code of conduct for all political parties participating in elections, thereby promoting good electoral conduct among them. The Commission further allowed civil society organisations to assist it in carrying out voter education and permitted them to participate in the preparations for the elections. It could be argued that the Commission was therefore able to deliver more credible elections to the Basotho in 2012 than was the case before. There have not been any complaints from the usual complainants about the electoral verdict. However, the Commission has still not been able to clean up the voters' roll. This remains an important concern for the Basotho and their political parties.

Political parties

Political parties are regarded as 'defining institutions of modern democracy' and 'a crucial link between citizens and government, and sources of governance for society in democratic systems'. As social formations, political parties are distinguishable from others by their primary purpose of seeking political power in order to govern. If they embrace democratic ethos and practices, they ought to offer spaces for citizens to participate in their activities. In Lesotho, political parties draw support from across all social groups and classes. Some parties even claim, without expressly excluding or including other social groups, to represent the workers. These are the Lesotho Workers Party (LWP) and the Popular Front for Democracy (PFD). Ordinary citizens participate in political processes mainly through their membership of political parties, and vote freely in national elections.

However, the 18 political parties registered with the IEC in Lesotho still face challenges, which affect their ability to work as effective instruments for political participation and democracy. They have been 'characterised by incessant intra-party and inter-party conflict and feuding sparked by personality clashes and power struggles'. They are formed with a remarkable degree of ease as a result of a lack of specific legislation governing their registration and regulation. Admittedly, a multi-party system should allow parties to form and work without hindrance, since this gives citizens a wide choice of parties they can join and participate in. However, these should be political parties with the capacity and clear intention to take over state power and rule. This is not the case in Lesotho. Each time the country approaches elections, new parties emerge as a result of splits in existing parties, which themselves are already organisationally weak and functionally ineffective as institutions befitting the label of political party. The primary objective of winning governmental power does not appear to guide the formation of parties in Lesotho. Instead, parties are formed by political elites as instruments for accessing Parliament and the lucrative benefits associated with it.

Motivated by gaining access to lucrative benefits, political parties in Lesotho therefore provide very little or no space for citizen participation in their policy-development processes and activities. This task remains the sole preserve of the leadership. General membership of political parties provides some space for participation through decision-making at annual general conferences. These forums are usually attended by delegates selected by the members at lower levels of individual party structures. In addition to discussing general policy issues, these forums also provide delegates with the opportunity to participate in the election of national executive committees in line with the constitutional provisions of each party. In cases where there are pressing and urgent issues that need immediate action, special conferences are called as per individual party constitutions and delegates selected accordingly. Notwithstanding these arrangements providing for participation by the membership in the affairs of parties, the leadership of Lesotho's political parties generally do not tolerate any form of dissent. In many cases, the leadership works hard to ensure that members holding and expressing views different from their own are not elected to influential positions within the party or are even made to leave the party.

The National Assembly Electoral Act, 2011, attempts to ensure that representation of women, the youth and people with disabilities in political activities is improved. This is done by encouraging all political parties registering with the IEC, for the purpose of contesting elections, to facilitate full participation of these groups on an equal basis by ensuring their free access to public political meetings, facilities and venues, by respecting their rights to freely communicate with political parties, and by generally refraining from forcing them to adopt a particular political position or to engage in, or refrain from engaging in, any political activity, other than out of their own free choice. There is a huge disjuncture, however, between these legal provisions and actual practice. Parties continue to demonstrate unwillingness to implement these affirmative-action policies. In the three main political parties for example – the Democratic Congress (DC), the

All Basotho Convention (ABC) and the BNP – leaders, deputies and secretary-generals are men over 35 years of age (the cut-off point for the youth). In the fourth party, the LCD, the leader and deputy are both men. It is only the position of secretary-general that is occupied by a woman. The main channel through which women and the youth participate in their respective parties' affairs is normally through the women's and youth leagues of these parties. There are, however, no groups representing people with disabilities that are structurally involved in the affairs of any political parties in Lesotho.

Although voters who are resident outside the country are legally allowed to vote, in practice they fail to do so. Arrangements are normally made to facilitate voting on site for staff of the country's embassies. This arrangement is, however, limited to embassy staff and does not include other groups such as migrant workers and students studying at institutions outside Lesotho. This means that these people are disenfranchised. On the whole, therefore, political parties in Lesotho demonstrate scope for promoting participation, but they also face challenges as instruments for fostering meaningful and effective participation.

Other weaknesses of political parties in the country include limited capacity due to lack of resources. Many of them do not have offices, because they simply cannot afford to run them. Consequently, those in power have enjoyed an unfair advantage over the opposition for many years, because they have had access to state resources and have used these to their advantage both during and between elections. Aware of this reality, the political elites recently agreed to state funding of political parties to ensure that they have some access to funds in order to run their offices. Parties qualify for this funding based on their electoral performance, as provided for under section 71 of the National Assembly Electoral Act, 2011. This is a positive development that should also be emulated by other countries in Africa, especially those characterised as one party dominant states.

The legislature

Participation in the legislative process in Lesotho takes several forms. The first, as everywhere else in democratic systems, is through elections. Those elected then participate in all forms of parliamentary processes and committees. Membership of the National Assembly and the Senate is fairly open to ordinary citizens of Lesotho, in terms of the Constitution and electoral law. Both these instruments provide that every person who is a registered voter and is able to speak, read and write Sesotho or English well enough to take an active part in the proceedings of both Houses of Parliament, and who is not incapacitated by physical disability, qualifies for membership of Parliament. These criteria have resulted in some candidates with very limited educational qualifications securing membership of Parliament, resulting in Members of Parliament (MPs) constrained by limited capacity and a generally poor level of parliamentary debate. The same situation applies to the Senate, where some of the Principal Chiefs face similar constraints.

For the ordinary citizen, participation in legislative processes is a relatively new phenomenon which has arisen from the introduction of parliamentary portfolio committees overseeing different ministries of government. These committees are seriously under-resourced. They have extremely limited research capacity and are forced to rely on the resources of Parliament as a whole. They can hardly seek out specialised expertise to enable them to propose amendments to laws and scrutinise government policy. Such services are usually provided by professional consultants for hefty fees, which the committees cannot afford. Ironically the executive – the very body which is being critically monitored – generally supplies the committees with the information they want. The committees operate on a consensus basis among members, but sometimes vote in order to reach decisions. Even after voting there are channels through which the views of detracting minorities can be heard when the business under consideration is tabled in Parliament. The committees criticise the government, as that is one of the main reasons for their establishment.

Parliament has opened avenues for different sectors of society to participate in law-making processes and the public is invited to make representations to relevant committees of Parliament. Recent examples of such consultations, although criticised as inadequate by civil society organisations (in terms of scope and time frames), were the Land Bill, 2009, and the National University of Lesotho (Amendment) Bill, 2011.

Other than parliamentary committees, citizens also have the opportunity to participate in the work of Parliament through links with their respective MPs at rallies that they organise in their respective constituencies, although there are complaints that this channel does not work as effectively as it should. This is because MPs do not go back to their voters as often as they should to consult with them, despite monthly allowances ranging from M400 to M600 (USD50- USD75), as well as other parliamentary allowances, to facilitate such work. MPs elected under the FPTP ballot are also each given a secretary. This secretary is recruited by the relevant MP, but is paid by Parliament. On the whole, therefore, avenues for public participation in parliamentary processes exist in Lesotho, but their effective implementation remains a challenge.

Local government structures

The local government system offers more space for citizens to participate than other levels of government. Unlike large and socially diverse countries, Lesotho has a unitary state with district, urban and community councils that function as sub-national units of government. The first local elections under the British colonial administration took place in 1960. These elections offered the Basotho the first opportunity to participate in the selection of their representatives. However, the elections were not based on the principle of universal suffrage. Women were not allowed to participate by way of voting and standing as candidates, because only tax-paying citizens (at that time only men) were accorded these rights. The district councils established after these elections were abolished by the BNP government in 1968.

It was only on 30 April 2000 that the LCD government again called local elections and re-established the local government system. These elections were different from those of the 1960s, in that they were based on full adult suffrage. One-third of the seats in all 129 councils were reserved for women in terms of section 18(a)(1A) of the Local Government Elections [Amendment] Act, 2004, to promote participation of women. Membership of the councils is open to all citizens, including two gazetted chiefs, who are nominated by other chiefs.

Although the political leadership introduced the MMP system for national elections in 2002 to ensure a more inclusive Parliament and in order to stop post-election conflict, it retained the FPTP system for local-government elections. It is not clear why the political elites found the MMP system unsuitable for local elections. The MMP would arguably create more room than the FPTP for participation of more political parties in the respective local councils, as it did at national level.

The Local Government Regulations, 2005, create space for citizens to participate in the activities of their respective councils. They can, if they so wish, request official documents of the councils, including minutes of their meetings, for a fee that councils may prescribe. They can also attend the meetings of the councils, except when confidential issues are discussed. However, the Basotho have not used these opportunities. They neither participate in the budgetary processes of their councils, nor do they make any submissions or inputs in the decision-making processes of councils. It is usually the councils and individual councillors who consult with the people through the centuries-old pitso system (general public gatherings open to all citizens). It is likely that citizens may not be using the legally established channels for participating in the activities of their respective councils because they do not know that these exist.

The country held the second round of local-government elections on 1 October 2011. The structure of these councils has now been changed by reducing the number of community councils from 128 to 65, probably to reduce expenditure in this sector of government. Other changes include the introduction of 11 urban councils and the retention of one municipal council for Maseru City. In other respects, membership of the councils has not been changed. However, the Basotho do not show much enthusiasm for local elections. Voter turnout in local elections has been marginal compared with parliamentary elections. In 2005, voter turnout was only 30. 28%, while, in 2011, it increased marginally to 32%. This is in contrast to parliamentary elections where the lowest turnout ever was 49% in 2007.

The local government system faces two main challenges. One is extreme lack of capacity to carry out their functions as provided for in the local government constitutive act. Since their establishment, the councils have not been able to perform their functions, because they do not have the resources to do so. The funds allocated by central government are extremely limited and hardly enable noteworthy service provision. Although the act provides for fundraising by each council by various means, including certain levies, whatever small monies they collect are taken by the central government. They also do not have bank accounts where they could keep their funds, despite the fact that this is provided for in the act. Although the act stipulates the functions the central government ought to have decentralised and passed on to the councils, this has not happened and different ministries of government still perform these functions. This appears to indicate lack of political commitment on the part of government to its policy of decentralisation and devolution of power.

The councils also suffer from a severe lack of autonomy from the central government. They are not able to make their own policies and implement them without interference from the central government. As a result of these factors, the councils are virtually incapacitated and unable to do much. It remains to be seen whether this scenario will change under the new coalition government.

Traditional authorities

Lesotho as a nation-state owes its genesis to the institution of chieftainship, which continues to enjoy a large degree of popular legitimacy and relevance despite the establishment of elected government. Every village, no matter how small or big, has its own chief. There are five categories of chiefs, namely 22 principal chiefs, 2 independent chiefs, 282 area chiefs, 235 chiefs and 695 headmen.

Ascension and succession to the office of chief are governed by the Laws of Lerotholi, which are codified customary practices, and the Chieftainship Act, 1968. According to the provisions of these laws, daughters of chiefs cannot succeed their fathers as chiefs – only the sons can. The practice presents problems of discrimination based on gender. However, this practice has its roots in Basotho culture, which reflects the patriarchal nature of the society. Attempts by activists seeking to promote gender parity between men and women and to change this practice have so far been unsuccessful. There is a case currently before the Court of Appeal in which a daughter of the late Principal Chief of Ha 'Mamathe is seeking to be recognised as the rightful successor to her late parents. The verdict is being awaited. However, women do succeed their husbands as chiefs until their sons come of age. In cases where there is no son to claim the position of chief, the wife of such a chief also succeeds her husband. It is after her death that the position moves to the next family male in line.

Chiefs below the level of Principal Chiefs are allowed to participate in politics. Indeed, many have successfully stood for election. This practice has the potential to undermine the supposed apolitical nature of the chieftainship. It pits chiefs against ordinary citizens for votes and political office. The chiefs may be interested in political positions because this is the only way in which they can earn better salaries. Political positions in Lesotho are more lucrative than many others, and furthermore do not require any special skills and qualifications. The only skill required is the ability to read and write Sesotho or English well enough in order to participate in proceedings.

The chieftainship as a whole is no different from other state institutions in terms of legal accountability. It answers directly to the Minister responsible for Local Government and Chieftainship Affairs. The Minister has overall powers to formally approve the selection of a new chief by the families concerned. The Minister further has powers to discipline any chief, which include suspension or removal from office. Chiefs also remain accountable to the people under their authority through their seniors within the chieftainship hierarchy and are subject to discipline by their seniors at different levels. If this mechanism does not produce the outcomes expected, the Minister can intervene and invoke appropriate legal provisions against any chief, including the Principal Chiefs.

In terms of public consultations, the chieftainship is by far the institution closest to the people in the villages, where even community councillors cannot exercise effective reach. Because of their proximity to the people, chiefs are able to call lipitso (c0mmon assemblies) to consult with their people on many matters affecting their communities. They perform a wide range of functions extending significantly beyond those listed in the Chieftainship Act, 1968. They do not observe formal working hours as other public officials do, and people often call on chiefs at night to resolve problems. Even commercial banks rely on the chiefs to attest to the residency credentials of clients. On the whole, the chieftainship continues to play important roles in the lives of the Basotho.

The biggest challenge the chiefs face is poor remuneration from the government. They do not receive salaries, but paltry allowances from as low as M400 (USD50) per month, when councillors receive M2 500 (USD312. 50) per month – more than six times this allowance. Of late, the government seems to be neglecting chiefs in terms of developing their capacities to execute their legal duties. The government has devoted time to training councillors in their duties, powers and responsibilities, but has left the chiefs out of these exercises. Consequently, for example, there is a problem on the part of some chiefs and ordinary Basotho in the villages regarding the exact role of the chiefs in matters of land allocation. This function is to be performed by the councils as per the Local Government Act, 1997, but many Basotho still look to their chiefs for this service. The councils themselves depend on the chiefs in cases where there are disputes related to land. The chiefs know who owns which pieces of land, livestock and other properties in every village. Councillors do not have such knowledge because of settlement patterns in Lesotho. Villages are scattered and each councillor is responsible for an electoral division, which covers a cluster of villages. As such, councillors are geographically removed from the people on the ground in these areas.

Development assistance and foreign relations

The legislative arm of the state in Lesotho has a limited role in foreign policy, including the signing of international agreements and treaties. Such issues are not subject to democratic debate in the legislature and remain the preserve of the executive. This effectively turns Parliament into a body that simply rubber-stamps executive decisions. Access to information relating to development assistance is scant and scattered, and not easily accessible from a single point of reference. Information has to be distilled from annual budget speeches made by the Minister of Finance to Parliament (available on the government website) and can also partly be accessed from the donor community, such as the United Nations Development Programme (UNDP) through its website. Complete and detailed information, however, is not available.

In keeping with the Paris Declaration on Aid Effectiveness, there appears to be a high level of cooperation and coordination among donors and with the government in terms of external financial resources made available to the country. Development partners generally do not impose conditionalities on the assistance they provide to the country. They work closely with the government under mutually agreed terms and on an analysis of how well funds have been used by the government in previous years. Several development partners, under the umbrella of the UNDP, provide capacity-building support in aid of democratic development. The main beneficiaries of such assistance have been the IEC, the Directorate on Corruption and Economic Offences (DCEO), the Office of the Ombudsman, Parliament and the Ministry of Justice. The UNDP has also provided assistance to civil society organisations. The main beneficiaries have been the TRC, which has received funds to engage with the media, youth organisations and political parties on projects that contribute to the achievement of the MDGs.

Conclusion and recommendations

Conditions exist and spaces are generally available for political participation in Lesotho since the country's return to multi-party politics in 1993. Democratic institutions fostering political participation operate reasonably well despite persistent challenges. Citizens, however, have no input in the development of public policies and national budgets. The government should open up these spaces to enable citizens to participate in public policy-making processes, including the preparation of the national budget, to ensure that these reflect the needs of citizens.

A partly liberalised media environment has led to an increase in the number of media outlets, giving citizens more diversified options for accessing information and expressing their opinions. However, the state-owned media still remains the monopoly and propaganda machinery of those in power. Citizens with views contrary to those of government, individually or as organisations, continue to be subject to various types of censorship. Opposition politicians are generally barred access to the airwaves controlled by the state broadcast media. Voices and parties critical of government only enjoy access to the state media by will of the government. The government should review all laws related to the media and repeal those which are outdated and inhibit media freedom. It should also transform the state-owned broadcasters into editorially independent public broadcasters to ensure uncensored access by all citizens and their organisations, including opposition political parties, to airwaves nationally.

Access to official information remains a big problem for citizens. Such access is not provided for the media, nor for citizens directly. There is no law giving citizens or the media the right of access to state-held information. The government should pass into law an updated and improved Access and Receipt of Information Bill, 2000, to provide such access and to effect transparency in government. Given that this bill may now be outdated, Parliament should invite citizens both individually and collectively through their different organisations to comment and provide suggestions on the content of the bill.

Lesotho has made huge advances through constitutional and electoral reforms, which resulted in the introduction of the MMP electoral system. The system led to important political outcomes such as an inclusive Parliament, political stability and, crucially, alternation of political power to a democratically elected coalition government. The IEC has also become a more transparent institution working much more closely with key stakeholders in all processes relating to elections. These reforms may serve as a useful example to other countries on the African continent.

However, the IEC must clean up the voters' roll to ensure that future elections are of a higher quality than in the past. Parliament should also amend electoral law to enable all citizens of Lesotho resident outside the country to vote.

A corrosive culture of persistent fragmentation continues to undermine the role of political parties as institutions facilitating political participation and democracy. Often engaged in unhelpful internal wrangling over power, they frequently split every time the country approaches elections. The legal framework for political parties is far too lax and leads to registration of many weak parties, which ultimately do not add value to democracy and political participation in Lesotho. There is a need for a new law designed exclusively to regulate the registration and operations of political parties.

Public participation in parliamentary processes is still low, partly because Parliament itself is still undergoing institutional reform, including efforts to streamline its newly established portfolio committee system. Parliament should do more to open itself to effective public participation through its portfolio committees, including the use of public hearings and written submissions on bills under consideration. It should have a regularly updated website on which all pending legislation, notices of the dates and deadlines in respect of hearings and submissions, and the postal and online addresses to which these have to be sent, should be posted. It should allocate more resources to itself and its portfolio committees to provide sufficient capacity for research. It should establish close links with civil society and continue with the good practice of consultation with communities and interest and expert groups before bills are passed.

Local authorities ought to become more effective channels of political participation, as they were established to function as such. However, they face challenges, including their lack of capacity and lack of autonomy from central government. The laws governing them allow for public participation in the processes of these structures, but, in practice, this does not happen because citizens are probably unaware that such avenues exist. The government should, in conformity with its decentralisation policy, allocate the requisite resources to councils in order to capacitate them, grant them autonomy to carry out their functions, and help to mobilise public campaigns to inform citizens about their rights of participation in local government affairs.

With their historically deep roots, traditional authorities still form an integral part of Basotho society, despite the introduction of elected structures of government. Their relevance and legitimacy remain largely unquestioned. However, the institution suffers from government neglect. The government should review the allowances of chiefs both as an incentive and in recognition of the valuable contribution they make to the lives of the Basotho in the villages. It should also include the chiefs in the same training it offers to councillors to improve their legal service delivery and liaison roles.

As is the case in other Southern African Development Community (SADC) countries, Parliament in Lesotho is weak relative to the power exercised by the executive branch of government. The executive signs important international agreements and treaties without these being debated in Parliament. Foreign policy issues and international agreements have profound and long-term consequences for any nation and it is crucial for these to be subjected to democratic debate in Parliament. The government should therefore consult Parliament before it signs international treaties and agreements so that these first obtain the blessing of the representatives of the people, and, in this way, acquire the status of mandated and legitimate policy.

Chapter One
Lesotho: Political Participation and Democracy

Main report

Introduction

This is a report on a study of political participation and democracy in Lesotho. As a concept, political participation may mean different things, depending on the context in which it is invoked. For the purposes of this report, the concept is used broadly to include citizen participation in local and national elections, both as voters and candidates, and citizen participation in public policy and decision-making processes. In this sense, political participation contains the elements of both republican and deliberative democratic theories. 1The report is divided into ten main sections (chapters) as proposed by the Africa Governance Monitoring and Advocacy Project (AfriMAP) Research Guide issued for this series of country reports. Each section (chapter) seeks to answer a set of questions reflected in the Guide. The first chapter provides the background and context of the report and outlines the major political, legal and other developments relevant to the process of political participation, including an overview of important constitutional changes. The second chapter deals with the constitutional framework and describes the legal framework of the state within which political participation is ensured under international law. The third chapter is devoted to equal citizenship, with a focus on how the Lesotho government is dealing with issues of citizenship and the extent to which this complies with international standards and commitments. The fourth chapter addresses participation in the policy process and captures the overall sense of depth in policy debate and the extent to which it is possible for citizens in general to participate in government and the development process. Chapter 5 looks at elections and the electoral process, as well as citizens' participation within the context of a number of relevant African standards. Chapter 6 focuses on political parties as the primary mechanism through which citizens can actively participate in national politics. Since the legislature is the most important institution for the expression of democratic debate, chapter 7 examines Lesotho's legislature. The process of democratisation would arguably not be complete without devolution of power to sub-national level, and Lesotho, too, has introduced a local government system as a mechanism for more accountable government. The local government system is explored in chapter 8.

Chapter 9 looks at traditional authorities and their role in Lesotho's political system, while chapter 10 reviews development assistance and foreign relations, and the extent to which they are subject to the rules of democratic accountability.

Background and context

From the formation of the Lesotho nation-state in the 1820s under the leadership of its founder, Moshoeshoe I, until the present, the Basotho are known to have practised the best form of popular democratic participation under the common assembly or pitso system (plural lipitso). Machobane highlights the centrality of the pitso system in Basotho society and notes that 'a ruler and his council might agree on a major issue of policy, but, ideally, and often in practice, he needed ... to put the matter before a pitso before implementing it'. It was, and still is, open to all citizens to express their views freely without any fear of retribution. After carefully listening to all sides of the debate, the chief, who usually chaired the proceedings, would summarise what had been said, add his own input and then proceed to create a consensus. This over-a-century-old system still characterises the lives of the Basotho in their respective communities. The institution is now used by the government to solicit public input on issues affecting their communities and to convey information from the government to the people in their respective villages.

A former British protectorate, along with Botswana and Swaziland, the Kingdom of Lesotho attained independence on 4 October 1966 and adopted the British-style, constitutional, monarchical parliamentary system, with a bicameral Parliament composed of the Senate made up of 33 members (22 Principal and Ward Chiefs and 11 other members who are nominated by the King). The National Assembly was composed of 60 Members of Parliament (MPs) elected in 1965 under the First-Past-The-Post (FPTP) voting system– a system in which a candidate who obtains the most votes (and not necessarily a majority of votes) is the winner. Although the parliamentary political system accorded the Basotho political participation with full citizenship, women were denied the right to vote, under the rules of the then 1959 Constitutional Handbook, in the first-ever elections of 1960 held for local government structures in the form of district councils. This Constitutional Handbook laid down criteria for people to qualify as voters, including the criterion that 'a voter should have paid tax at any time during the five years immediately preceding his registration as an elector'. This provision effectively disenfranchised women, as they did not pay tax in the form of 'hut tax' imposed by the colonial state on males over the age of 21. Women were also regarded as minors under the customary and common laws governing the territory. 6 Thus political participation of women was legally proscribed under the 1959 Constitutional Handbook which granted the franchise to the Basotho.

Following lengthy constitutional talks (1958–1966), the new Constitution came into force on 30 April 1965, and it was in terms of this framework that the first parliamentary elections were held. The new Constitution, in chapter II, provided protection of fundamental human rights and freedoms, including, for the purpose of this study, freedom of expression and freedom of assembly and association. It also broadened the scope for political participation by citizens in Lesotho by granting a right to vote and a right to stand for election, with the following exceptions:

No person shall be qualified to be registered as an elector in elections to the National Assembly who, at the date of his application to be registered (a) is, by virtue of his own act, under any acknowledgement of allegiance, obedience or adherence to any foreign power or state; or (b) is under sentence of death imposed on him by any court in Lesotho; or (c) is, under any law in force in Lesotho, adjudged or otherwise declared to be of unsound mind. 8Similarly, for candidates for National Assembly elections, section 44(2) of the Constitution provided that no one would qualify to stand for elections if he was not a citizen of Lesotho, registered as a voter, and was able to speak, read and write either English or Sesotho 'well enough to take an active part in the proceedings of the National Assembly'. In relation to gender equity, the new Constitution improved on the past by at least giving women a right to vote in elections. The pre-independence elections were held in 1965 and were contested by the first three political parties under the FPTP voting system inherited from the departing British colonial administration. The parties were the Basotho National Party (BNP), formed in 1959, the Basutoland Congress Party (BCP), established in 1952, and the Marematlou Freedom Party (MFP), which was established as a result of a merger between the Marematlou Party and the Freedom Party in 1962. The BNP won the poll and became the first post-colonial government of Lesotho by a narrow margin of two seats in a 60-member Parliament, while its arch rival, the BCP, won 25 seats, with the MFP winning four seats. 10The BNP's rule came to an end as per the provisions of the 1965 Constitution after a five- year period when the second elections were held in January 1970. At these elections, the Prime Minister realised that his party was losing when the election results were being announced by the Electoral Office on the state-owned Radio Lesotho. The results received and announced by the

Electoral Office showed that the BCP was winning the poll. According to Khaketla, the results were as follows: the BCP – 35 constituencies; the BNP – 23; and the MFP – 1. But these results were never made public, since the BNP government ordered the Electoral Office to stop announcing them. The Prime Minister then moved swiftly to annul the process on Radio Lesotho on Friday, 30 January 1970. He claimed that his government had been forced to take drastic action by widespread acts of violence and intimidation instigated by BCP supporters against his party's members and electoral officers. He declared a state of emergency, suspended the country's Constitution, placed King Moshoeshoe II under house arrest, and detained opposition leaders without trial, including Ntsu Mokhekhe of the BCP and Bernard Makalo Khaketla of the MFP.

He also declared 'a five-year moratorium on politics, stating that the Westminster system was not in tune with Lesotho's traditions and would [...] need to be adapted and modified to meet Lesotho's special requirements'. The allegations of violence and intimidation were alleged to have been untruthful. The Prime Minister had earlier announced over Radio Lesotho that the 'elections had been conducted in an atmosphere of peace and quiet throughout the country'. He convened an urgent Cabinet meeting to prepare to hand over power to the victorious BCP, but he was pressurised by his Cabinet members, notably his reactionary deputy, Chief Sekhonyana 'Maseribane and Chief Peete Nkuebe Peete, to seize power by force. The two ministers did not want to see a change of government, because, according to Leeman, they dreaded the prospect of being charged for their criminal activities during the voting process. Leeman surmises that Peete had ordered his supporters to shoot the BCP supporters in his home constituency of Koeneng, while 'Maseribane had forced his BCP opponent at gunpoint to reverse the results after losing the elections in his constituency. But Leeman's version of events was strongly disputed by a number of participants at a Validation Workshop held to critique the draft version of this report. These included current members of the BNP and its splinter party, the Basotho Democratic National Party (BDNP). They argued that Chief Sekhonyana 'Maseribane would not have forced anyone to 'reverse' the results of the poll, because the BNP had won all but one of the five constituencies in the Quthing District. They argued that 'Maseribane himself had won his constituency. The controversies surrounding this period notwithstanding, the result of these events was that all forms of democratic political participation were proscribed, as the Prime Minister also declared a five-year moratorium on politics.

In 1973, the Prime Minister established a 93-member Interim National Assembly (INA) to draft a new constitution which would be 'in tune with Lesotho's traditions'. Although the INA was dominated by the BNP, this body reflected a broader spectrum of political opinion in the country and included some senior members of the BCP, including its Deputy Leader, Mr GP Ramoreboli, who led a breakaway faction of the BCP. 17 The BCP leader and his supporters, on the other hand, demanded a true coalition government, to which the BNP could not agree. The BCP even attempted to overthrow the BNP regime by force, but could not succeed, as it was poorly organised. 19The term of the INA lasted until 1985, when the BNP regime called the third elections since 1965. These elections were boycotted by the opposition parties in protest against the stringent conditions imposed on opposition parties by the BNP regime. These conditions made it virtually impossible for the opposition to participate in the elections. The BNP regime, however, was ousted from power on 20 January 1986 by the military, which ruled the country for seven years (1986–1993). Under Lesotho Order 1 of 1986, the military junta, like its predecessor, established a system completely devoid of democratic political participation. This instrument became Lesotho's constitutional framework and gave the King legislative and executive powers, which he was to exercise in accordance with the advice of a six-person-strong Military Council (composed of the Commander of the Lesotho Defence Force [LDF] and Chairperson, Major-General Justin Metsing Lekhanya, and other senior military officers). The advice of the Military Council was, however, mandatory and the King was in no position to refuse. The military junta also introduced Lesotho Order 4 of 1986, which banned all political activity.

This meant that democratic political participation was effectively proscribed until 1992, when civil society organisations (CSOs) and the international donor community exerted enormous internal pressure on the military regime to establish a National Constituent Assembly (NCA). The NCA, an advisory body to the military junta, was tasked with making recommendations on a new constitution, which would return the country to civilian rule. The NCA was composed of 107 members drawn from different sections of society, namely: 17 members of the government, 20 District Development Councillors, the 22 Principal Chiefs, 20 recognised politicians, ten representatives of the public interest appointed by the Military Council, eight members of the armed forces, and ten representatives of urban councils. The two main political parties, the BNP and the BCP, had, along with other smaller parties, initially rejected the NCA out of uncertainty as to how the 20 recognised politicians would be selected and out of fear that the body would be dominated by the members of the military regime. They would probably not have relented their stance had the British High Commission not persuaded them to come on board. The BNP had its own troubles; its acting leader, Chief Matete Majara, was embroiled in leadership squabbles with others following the death of the party's leader, Chief Leabua Jonathan, in October 1986. The NCA used the 1966 Constitution as a basis for drafting a new constitution, but proposed several amendments, principal among which was the establishment of a number of key institutions. There was to be a Defence Commission made up of senior members of the military, the police and the intelligence service. This Commission would be consulted by the Prime Minister in appointing the Commanding Officer of the LD as an ex officio member of a new Cabinet. This effectively meant that the military would have powers to veto some decisions of government through this officer. Also to be established was a Council of State made up of judges, members of the opposition, and commanders of the military and police forces, which would have to approve a decision by the Prime Minister to declare a state of emergency. It would also have powers to appoint and remove the Prime Minister. Even the King would only be able to exercise his powers through the government or through the Council of State. 23 These amendments were clearly intended to limit the powers of both the Prime Minister and the King, because the military feared that these two would take actions (as they had in the past) that would plunge the country into another crisis similar to that of 1970. Most importantly, the military sought to protect its members against possible prosecution by a new civilian government. 24Other than these amendments, the NCA adopted the 1966 Constitution largely unchanged in other respects. This is relevant to issues of political participation, in that the Senate was left untouched, the FPTP electoral system was scarcely debated, and the Bill of Rights clause was retained. Thus, the transitional process had an inclusive character, in that the key actors in Lesotho's politics, notably the security establishment, the chieftainship and prominent politicians, had their interests safeguarded in the new Constitution. Major General Lekhanya announced that the new Constitution would be adopted in early 1991 and that elections would be called in June 1992. But the power struggle within the Military Council and general discontent among the rank and file of the military over pay rises and working conditions, coupled with popular dissatisfaction, industrial unrest and protests, forced Lekhanya out of power. He was replaced by Colonel P Ramaema, who was the most senior officer remaining within the Military Council after an earlier exit from power by two close relatives of the King (Colonels Sekhobe Letsie and Thaabe Letsie). Ramaema made it clear that the military was still determined to hand over power to civilian authority and took steps in that direction. These steps included the establishment of a Constitutional Commission with a mandate to solicit popular opinion on the new draft

Constitution and the recommendations of the NCA. The Commission was largely inclusive and representative of different sections of the population. Other than members of the NCA, it included representatives of seven registered political parties. It undertook its work from October 1991 to March 1992 and travelled throughout the country to hear public opinion. It convened about 66 meetings and received both oral and written submissions from the public. Despite dissatisfaction on the part of some social formations such as non-governmental organisations (NGOs), trade unions and churches over its slow pace and the military junta's reluctance to announce the election dates, the Commission managed to finish its work. Subsequently, the military junta paved the way for electoral processes to commence by lifting the ban on political activity. The country then held general elections on 23 March 1993 under the same FPTP voting system and the new 1993 Constitution, which provided for universal adult franchise, for a Bill of Rights protecting fundamental human rights, and for democratic participation. The BCP scooped all parliamentary seats in a now 65-member National Assembly.

The BNP contested the outcome in the courts of law, but lost all its cases.

The country's transitional period, especially after the 1993 poll and the next poll in 1998, proved even more turbulent than the earlier events described above. This period was characterised by several ugly episodes, including a 'palace coup d'état' carried out by King Letsie III, who was angered by the BCP government's refusal to reinstate his father, King Moshoeshoe II, who had been dethroned by the Lekhanya regime. There were also mutinies in the police and prisons services over pay rises, teachers' strikes over salary increases and, most importantly, internal wrangling within the ruling BCP, which led to the first major split in the party in June 1997. This resulted in the assumption of state power by the new splinter party, the Lesotho Congress for Democracy (LCD), under the leadership of the BCP leader and Lesotho's Prime Minister, Ntsu Mokhehle. The takeover of state power by the LCD and the concomitant relegation of the BCP to opposition ranks in Parliament caused a huge popular outcry about the legality and morality of this unelected change of government. The legal dimension of the argument, however, proved difficult to pursue, as the Constitution of Lesotho 1993 did not prohibit such a move. The LCD consequently completed the remaining term of Parliament and government as ruling party. The moral dimension still characterises Lesotho's politics to date and the population is still highly critical when MPs cross the floor in Parliament. The next elections were held in 1998 under the same FPTP electoral model. The LCD repeated the electoral performance of its predecessor, the BCP in 1993, by winning the vote by a landslide, taking all but one of the now 80 seats in the enlarged Parliament. The joint opposition, made up of the BNP, MFP, BCP and other smaller parties, engaged in massive protests, rejecting the electoral verdict as fraudulent. They proceeded to the Royal Palace where they set up camp and called on the King to dissolve Parliament and the LCD government and to call another election under a Proportional Representation (PR) electoral system (an electoral system in which the allocation of parliamentary seats to political parties is proportional to the overall number of votes they receive).

The King could not heed these calls, as they were unconstitutional. The opposition parties became frustrated and embarked on various acts of protest, including mounting roadblocks to prevent public servants and other workers from reaching their workplaces. The Lesotho security forces appeared to be either overwhelmed or reluctant to disperse the protesters. Consequently, the embattled Prime Minister and the new leader of the LCD, who had taken over from the ailing Mokhehle, called on South Africa under the banner of the official sub-regional intergovernmental organ, the Southern African Development Community (SADC), of which Lesotho is a member, to intervene militarily to restore law and order. South African military forces, along with their Botswana counterparts, entered Lesotho to restore some stability so as to allow negotiations between the LCD government and the opposition parties under the auspices of the SADC.

As part of the mediation effort, the SADC dispatched a commission led by South African Constitutional Court judge, Justice Pius Langa, to investigate the opposition's claims of vote-rigging by the LCD and to make appropriate recommendations to resolve the ensuing impasse. The result of this effort was that no fraud was established, but some serious irregularities were nevertheless found to have occurred. The main problem was identified as the FPTP electoral system, which excluded most of the losing political parties from Parliament. The Commission recommended, among other measures to resolve the crisis, that Lesotho review its electoral system under a new body, the Interim Political Authority, made up of two representatives from each of the 12 political parties that had taken part in the elections. As a consequence, some constitutional and electoral reforms were made in order to introduce a more inclusive voting system – the Mixed Member Proportional (MMP) system.

The main difference between the proportional and parallel (in this case the FPTP) system is that the former produces outcomes that generally tend to benefit smaller parties. Parties winning more constituency votes receive fewer, and perhaps even no, votes in respect of the PR seats, based on their total share of the overall votes. Caramani captures this issue thus:

The list [PR] seats are awarded in such a way as to rectify the under- representation created in the constituencies, ensuring that a party's overall number of seats (not just its list seats) is proportional to its vote share. Typically, small parties fare badly in the singe-member constituencies, winning hardly any seats, while the larger parties, which usually win more than their 'fair share' in the constituencies, are awarded few or none of the list [PR] seats because their constituency seats alone bring them up to or close to the total number to which they are entitled. 26 [Emphasis added]

By the same token, the parallel system generates outcomes that favour big parties. According to Caramani, there is a separation between the list or PR component and its constituency counterpart in the allocation of seats in that:

The list seats are awarded to parties purely on the basis of their list votes, without taking any account of what happened in the constituencies. This benefits large parties, which retain the over-representation they typically achieve in the constituencies, and offers less comfort to smaller ones than a compensatory system would do. 27 [Emphasis added]

The first outcome was witnessed in Lesotho during the 2002 elections, where the LCD could not obtain any PR seats because it had won 79 out of 80 constituency-based seats. 28 Aware of this otherwise unfavourable eventuality and motivated by a desire to maintain its dominance in Parliament, the LCD was unhappy about the introduction of the MMP model and, instead, preferred the Mixed Member Parallel model. 29 However, it was eventually forced by pressure from external forces, in particular the SADC, to compromise and accept the MMP system. 30 According to the new voting system, Lesotho retained its 80 electoral constituencies, but a further 40 additional seats based on the PR party lists were created. The country then proceeded to hold a new election in 2002 under the MMP system.

The system produced a positive political outcome, in that at least ten of the main parties secured representation in the National Assembly, and the country subsequently enjoyed some degree of political stability between 2002 and 2007. However, due to continuing in-fighting and power struggles within the ruling LCD, the party suffered another split in October 2006, when one of the party's prominent members and long-term civil servant from the era of the British colonial administration through all the successive governments up to that time, crossed the floor to form a new party, the All Basotho Convention (ABC). Seemingly in a response to the emergence of the ABC, the Prime Minister,

Pakalitha Mosisili, called a snap election, which was held on 17 February 2007.

The new ABC put up a remarkable and unprecedented performance in the country's post- 1993 transitional electoral history. It won all the constituencies in the major urban areas in the northern part of the country and secured 17 seats in the now greatly enlarged 120-seat National Assembly. The ruling LCD managed to hang on to the largely rural-based constituencies in the southern parts of the country. The introduction of the MMP system and its wide acclaim as the most 'innovative step' in ensuring inclusivity of all political parties and in stemming political conflict and rivalry, was however soon to be dissipated. The political elite from the ruling LCD and the main ABC opposition undermined the MMP by contesting the 2007 poll on the basis of unregulated pre-election alliances and coalitions with minor partners. Their primary aim was to secure as many seats as they could under the PR component of the voting system.

The main parties entered into agreements with their smaller partners to compile a common list of candidates drawn from both sides of the PR party lists and to let the smaller partners contest the party seats, while the main parties contested the constituency-based seats. In both cases, the supporters of all these parties were coached to vote for the bigger parties on the constituency ballot and the smaller partners on the PR ballot. This arrangement produced the results expected by party engineers. The Independent Electoral Commission (IEC) was, according to its then Chairperson, Mr Leshele Thoahlane, hamstrung by the electoral law, since it did not prevent the formation of such alliances. The Commission did, however, warn leaders of political parties about the palpable danger these alliances posed to the MMP system. This warning was ignored by the leaders. 34The result was to spark a new form of election-related dispute over on the allocation of PR seats. The IEC treated these alliances as separate political parties, rather than the integrated coalitions that they really were. This allowed them undue advantage over the rest of the parties participating in these elections. Attempts by the MFP to challenge this allocation of seats through the High Court became extremely complicated and technical and were ultimately resolved on legal–technical grounds and not on substantive grounds. The High Court ruled that the MFP had no legal status to challenge the allocation of seats, since the electoral law expressly stated that only voters or candidates had a right to take election-related cases to court. This law, however, was passed to govern the old FPTP electoral system, and was not amended to support the new MMP model. The High Court also recommended that Parliament make further constitutional and electoral reforms to deal with this problem. These steps were taken by Parliament and a new National Assembly Electoral Act, 2011, was accordingly passed and implemented during the next elections on 26 May 2012.

Conclusion

This chapter has attempted to sketch important political developments in Lesotho since independence, including constitutional and electoral reforms, which saw the introduction of a new electoral system, the MMP system. The model has proved to be a useful instrument for promoting political stability through the inclusion of more political parties in Parliament and thereby the inclusion of more political voices and views. Political participation has therefore been deepened in Lesotho. Although the main political parties effectively undermined the model through unregulated party-political alliances in the 2007 election, the new National Assembly Electoral Act, 2011, holds out the promise of protecting this model in future. The act provides, in section 55 that 'during general elections, constituency votes shall be counted both for the candidate and converted into party votes'. There were no further palpable threats to the model during the 2012 elections.

Chapter Two

Constitutional framework: TheConstitutionand international standards

Lesotho is a state party to a number of major international conventions, declarations and treaties relating to democracy and political participation. At international level, these instruments include the International Covenant on Civil and Political Rights, 1966, which Lesotho ratified on 9 December 1992. Article 25 of the Covenant provides that:

Every citizen shall have the right and the opportunity:

1. To take part in the conduct of public affairs, directly or through freely chosen representatives;

2. To vote and to be elected at genuine elections which shall be by universal and equal suffrage and shall be held by secret ballot, guaranteeing the free expression of the will of the electors;

Lesotho also ratified the International Convention on the Elimination of All Forms of Racial Discrimination in 1966. This provides, under article 7, that:

States Parties undertake to adopt immediate and effective measures, particularly in the fields of teaching, education, culture and information, with a view to combating prejudices which lead to racial discrimination and to promoting understanding, tolerance and friendship among nations and racial or ethnic groups,....

On 22 August 1995, Lesotho also ratified the Convention on the Elimination of All Forms of Discrimination against Women, 1979. The instrument seeks to eliminate all forms of discrimination against women, and, in article 7, provides:

States Parties shall take all appropriate measures to eliminate discrimination against women in the political and public life of the country and, in particular, shall ensure to women, on equal terms with men, the right:

1. To vote in all elections and public referenda and to be eligible for election to all publicly elected bodies;

2. To participate in formulation of government policy and the implementation thereof and to hold public office and perform all public functions at all levels of government;

3. To participate in non-governmental organizations and associations concerned with the public and political life of the country.

At continental level, the country has ratified the following instruments relevant to political participation: the African Charter on Human and Peoples' Rights, 1981, ratified on 10 February 1992; and the Protocol to the African Charter on Human and Peoples' Rights on the Rights of Women in Africa, 2003. Article 13 of the African Charter provides that 'Every citizen shall have the right to participate freely in the government of his country, either directly or through a freely chosen representative in accordance with the provisions of the law.' Article 9 of the Protocol provides as follows:

1. States Parties shall take specific positive action to promote participative governance and the equal participation of women in the political life of their countries through affirmative action, enabling national legislation and other measures to ensure that:

    a) women participate without any discrimination in all elections;

    b) women are represented equally at all levels with men in all electoral processes;

c) women are equal partners with men at all levels of development and implementation of State policies and development programmes.

States Parties shall ensure increased and effective representation and participation of women at all levels of decision-making. On 30 June 2010, Lesotho also ratified the African Charter on Democracy, Elections and Governance, 2007. The Charter commits state parties to its implementation according to the following principles, among others:

Holding of regular, transparent, free and fair elections; Promotion of gender equality in public and private institutions;

Effective participation of citizens in democratic and development processes and in governance of public affairs;

Strengthening political pluralism and recognising the role, rights and responsibilities of legally constituted political parties, including opposition political parties, which should be given a status under national law. Article 8 provides for the elimination of all forms of discrimination and commits state parties to legislative and administrative corrective measures. It reads:

State Parties shall eliminate all forms of discrimination, especially those based on political opinion, gender, ethnic, religious and racial grounds as well as any other form of intolerance.

State Parties shall adopt legislative and administrative measures to guarantee the rights of women, ethnic minorities, migrants, people with disabilities, refugees and displaced persons and other marginalised and vulnerable social groups.

State Parties shall respect ethnic, cultural and religious diversity, which contributes to strengthening democracy and citizen participation.

Under article 17, state parties reaffirm their commitment 'to regularly holding transparent, free and fair elections in accordance with the Union's Declaration on the Principles Governing Democratic Elections in Africa' and to:

1. Establish and strengthen independent and impartial national electoral bodies responsible for the management of elections.

2. Establish and strengthen national mechanisms that redress election-related disputes in a timely manner.

3. Ensure fair and equitable access by contesting parties and candidates to state controlled media during elections.

4. Ensure that there is a binding code of conduct governing legally recognized political stakeholders, government and

other political actors prior, during and after elections. The code shall include a commitment by political stakeholders to accept the results of the election or challenge them through... exclusively legal channels.

However, Lesotho has only acceded to the Convention against Torture and other Cruel, Inhuman and Degrading Treatment or Punishment, 1984 (which it did on 12 November 2001), but has not ratified it. The reason given for this at the time was that 'the instrument of ratification is being prepared'. Accession to treaties has a similar legal effect as ratification, but the two processes differ, in that, by acceding to a treaty, 'states accept the offer or opportunity to become a party to an already negotiated and signed treaty by other states'. On the other hand, ratification refers to a process whereby states indicate their 'consent to be bound to a treaty'. It gives states some time to domesticate the treaty through enacting necessary legislation to give effect to the treaty. The key difference is that accession has to do with acceptance of the treaty, while ratification binds parties to it.

At the sub-regional level, Lesotho is a member of the Southern African Development Community (SADC), and has ratified the following key instruments relating to democracy and political participation. The first instrument is the Treaty of the Southern African Development Community, 2001, which provides, under article 4(c) that the 'SADC and its Member States shall act in accordance with the following principles: [...] c) human rights, democracy and the rule of law'. Article 5 sets out the objectives of the SADC as being, among others, to 'promote common political values, systems and other shared values which are transmitted through institutions which are democratic, legitimate and effective'. The Treaty also commits member states to 'consolidate, defend and maintain democracy, peace, security and stability' in the region. The second instrument is the SADC Principles and Guidelines Governing Democratic Elections, 2004. The instrument commits member states to adhere to the following principles in conducting elections:

- Full participation of the citizens in the political process; Freedom of association;

- Political tolerance;

- Regular intervals for elections as provided for by the respective National Constitutions; Equal opportunity for all political parties to access the state media;

- Equal opportunity to exercise the right to vote and be voted for; Independence of the judiciary and impartiality of the electoral institutions; Voter education; and

- Acceptance of, and respect for, the election results by political parties proclaimed to have been free and fair by the competent national electoral authorities in accordance with thelawoftheland.

The third instrument is the SADC Protocol on Gender and Development, 2008, which commits state parties to promoting gender equality and equity by 2012. Articles 2, 12 and 13 are the most relevant to this project. Article 2(1)(a) provides that 'States Parties shall harmonise national legislation, policies, strategies and programmes with relevant regional and international instruments related to the empowerment of women and girls for purposes of ensuring gender equality and equity'. In the same spirit, article 12(1) reads: 'States Parties shall endeavour that, by 2015, at least fifty percent of decision-making positions in the public and private sectors are held by women'. Article 13 seeks to promote equal participation by men and women in electoral processes, and specifically provides that, 'States Parties shall adopt specific legislative measures and other strategies to enable women to have equal opportunities with men to participate in all electoral processes including the administration of elections and voting'. The extent to which Lesotho has conformed to these instruments will be reflected throughout the relevant parts of

Development of the Constitution

To a large degree, the legitimacy of the Constitution has been questioned by those in power more than by other actors. This may not be surprising; constitutions are intended to limit the powers of governments and, when Lesotho's constitutional provisions would not allow the excesses of the Basotho National Party (BNP) following the 1970 elections, the regime suspended it. Similarly, the military junta could not, by its very nature, use the Constitution as its guiding instrument or as 'a ground norm'. These two regimes prohibited political participation; the former by declaring 'a five-year moratorium on politics', which eventually led to over two decades of authoritarianism, and the latter by denying the Basotho a right to participate in matters concerning who should rule them for 7 years (1986–1993) through Lesotho Order 4 of 1986.

The current Constitution of 1993, which does not depart significantly from that of 1966 on key democratic principles, including entrenched fundamental human rights, was adopted after fairly consultative processes in which the main political actors participated, and can therefore be regarded as legitimate. Several constitutional amendments have been effected since the 1993 transition in order to address stubborn problems associated with electoral outcomes. These have largely been based on democratic processes in Parliament, and, as of now, there are no calls for constitutional change. Similarly, there are no constitutional cases pending in the courts of law.

Lesotho is a unitary state, which is divided for administrative purposes into ten districts. It introduced a local government system in 2005 when the first local elections were held. The local government system is similar to the national system in terms of composition; it has elected local councillors and representatives of the chiefs, who are nominated by other chiefs for two reserved seats per council. As is the case with parliamentary systems, Lesotho has three branches of government – the legislature, the executive and the judiciary, with each performing its constitutionally defined role. However, there is no clear institutional separation between the legislature and the executive as there is, for example, in the American system. Members of the executive must be drawn from the legislature in terms of the Constitution. Referendums are provided for in the Constitution when entrenched clauses of the Constitution are to be amended. However, there have never been any referendums in Lesotho since independence. The High Court of Lesotho has played a role in two recent cases; one related to matters of citizenship and another on political participation. The highlights of these cases are reflected in case studies 1 and 2 below.

The dual-citizenship case of Pholoana Adam Lekhoaba

There has been litigation around issues of citizenship and invariably political participation based on section 41 of the national Constitution. This section prohibits dual citizenship for Lesotho citizens. In the run-up to the 2007 parliamentary elections, the owner of a local radio station, Harvest FM, the reverend Pholoana Adam Lekhoaba, was deported on several occasions by the state on the grounds that he held south African citizenship. The state argued that, in terms of section 41(2)(b), Lekhoaba should have renounced his south African citizenship after attaining the age of 21, which he did not do. on the other hand, Lekhoaba argued that he was a citizen of Lesotho, by virtue of his birth, in terms of section 37 of the Constitution. He claimed to have been born in Lesotho in 1970, a fact established by the High Court. Lekhoaba was born in

Thaba-Tseka Ha Moqekela in Lesotho, where his relatives are still found, but his parents fled to south Africa during the political disturbances of the early 1970s. He consequently grew up in south Africa, where he eventually acquired citizenship.

In the run-up to the 2007 elections, he returned to Lesotho and established a private radio station in partnership with his wife, who was also a Lesotho citizen. The state charged the station's journalists with broadcasting inflammatory information and accused them of sedition. It also prevented the station from broadcasting for months. The so-called inflammatory and seditious information consisted in the station giving a platform to opposition parties to air their views and to conduct political analysis and debates.

In defending his stay in Lesotho and his dual-citizenship status, and highlighting the inconsistency of the state in handling the matter, Lekhoaba revealed that Lesotho's Prime Minister at the time, Pakalitha Mosisili, had a south African identification document, which he had acquired while teaching in that country's universities. Invoking section 41 of the national Constitution, which prohibits dual citizenship, Lekhoaba publicised this information on his radio station, arguing that it was not right for a person with a foreign identification document to rule Lesotho. He was therefore regarded by the state as causing instability and was deported from the country.

Political participation and gender empowerment/discrimination

There was a case in 2005 in which a Mosotho male, Mr Molefi T'šepe, challenged the provisions of the Local Government Elections (Amendment) Act, 2004, in the High Court of Lesotho on the grounds that the act was in conflict with section 18 of the Constitution, which prohibits discrimination in all its forms – including, for the purposes of this case, discrimination based on sex. The act reserved one-third of all local council seats for women to ensure higher representation of women in the local government system and to address gender imbalances in Lesotho. This meant that men were not allowed to stand for elections in some designated electoral divisions. Mr Tšepe wanted to stand for election in his electoral division, which was one of those earmarked for women. When the Independent Electoral Commission would not allow him to stand in the election in line with the provisions of the act, he took the Commission to the High Court and challenged the constitutionality of this act.

The court ruled that the Constitution did not prevent measures intended to give advantage to certain groups, such as women, who are under-represented in Lesotho's public life. It said the local government elections provided a good opportunity to address historical gender imbalances, and the purpose of the reservation of seats for women was further to ensure that Lesotho complied with its international obligations. The court therefore regarded the measure as positive discrimination and Mr T'šepe lost the case. The state was at pains to explain to the nation that Mosisili did not have south African citizenship, but had only acquired permanent residency status in that country. Lekhoaba threatened to disclose more people in top positions in the Lesotho government with south African identification documents and citizenship or residency. Lekhoaba fell ill during the legal battle and died in south Africa in January 2009 before his case could be decided by the High Court of Lesotho. The court later ruled that Lekhoaba was a citizen of Lesotho and was entitled to all the rights of citizens. The case therefore set a precedent in the courts of law regarding the issue of dual citizenship. However, the High Court also recommended that the constitutional clause on dual citizenship be reviewed by Parliament. There was a general public outcry after the case, especially from the ranks of the opposition, that the Constitution had to be amended to give all Basotho people a right to dual citizenship in countries of their own choice. Parliament, however, has yet to amend the Constitution based on this ruling. At the time of writing, it is still unconstitutional for the Basotho to have dual citizenship.

There have been no other legal contests regarding similar matters in Lesotho. The case may have opened up more avenues for women to participate in the political life of the country. In fact, the 58% representation of women in local Councils in 2005 surpassed the SADC quota of 30%.

Conclusion and recommendations
Lesotho is a state party to the main international treaties and conventions concerning democracy and political participation.

The Constitution of Lesotho contains adequate provisions for the protection of fundamental human rights, including rights to political participation and gender equity. However, the country has not ratified the Convention against Torture and Other Cruel, Inhuman and Degrading Treatment or Punishment, 1984, and should do so. It should also amend the Constitution to allow dual citizenship for the Basotho.

Chapter Three

Equalcitizenship

Lesotho is a state party to the main international and African human rights treaties relating to non-discrimination and equal citizenship. In this regard, it has ratified, among others, the following instruments: the UN Convention on the Protection of the Rights of All Migrant Workers and Members of their Families, ratified on 16 September 2005, the UN Convention on the Reduction of Statelessness, ratified on 24 September 2004, the OAU Convention Governing the Specific Aspects of Refugee Problems in Africa, ratified on 30 December 1988, and the Protocol on the Free Movement of Persons in the Southern African Development Community (SADC), ratified on 18 August 2005. The Constitution of Lesotho, 1993, accords equal citizenship to all Basotho. Chapter IV of the Constitution defines persons who are citizens and consequently accords them all citizenship rights, including the right of political participation. These include those who were citizens before the coming into force of the Constitution under the Lesotho Citizenship Order, 1971, and those who were born in Lesotho after the Constitution came into operation, with a proviso that the parents of such persons are themselves citizens of Lesotho. It further provides that even those who were born outside Lesotho, but whose parents are citizens of Lesotho, qualify to be Lesotho citizens, as well as women who are married to citizens of Lesotho, even after the death of such spouses. The Constitution, however, does not accord Lesotho citizenship to persons who, after the attainment of the age of 21, become citizens of other countries, unless they renounce citizenship of such other countries. The Refugee Act, 1983, recognises people who are refugees, provides for their application for refugee status, and sets out their rights and duties in line with international instruments (in this case, the OAU Convention Governing the Specific Aspects of Refugee Problems in Africa). It further provides for their ultimate acquisition of permanent residence and citizenship through the process of naturalisation, after at least five years of lawful residency in Lesotho. It also provides for participation in all these processes regarding application for refugee status and acquisition of Lesotho citizenship by representatives of the United Nations High Commission for Refugees. The act is fairly friendly to refugees and other aliens in Lesotho. It is not easy to establish the actual number of long-term residents excluded from citizenship, because of poor record-keeping within the Department of Immigration. However, the Director of Immigration indicated that the Department was inundated with large numbers of applicants for permanent residence and citizenship, and that over three-quarters of them qualify. The five-year period they are required to legally reside in Lesotho in order to qualify for citizenship is considered far too short in the opinion of this official. The government is considering lengthening this period. The Department has to carefully consider all applications in the context of contemporary challenges, including international crime and terrorism. The laws regulating aliens are regarded as too old and in need of review, because some people have abused Lesotho's citizenship to commit illegal activities in foreign countries. Those applying for refugee status and who have their applications rejected by the Minister have a right to seek a review by the High Court.

Non-discrimination and affirmative action

As already indicated, the Constitution, 1993, prevents any form of discrimination, but, for the purpose of this part of the report, it is important to indicate some specific steps that the country has taken to remedy inequalities based on gender. These steps include the provision in the National Assembly Electoral Act, 2011, that political parties submitting a list of candidates for proportional representation seats must ensure the inclusion of women on such lists, and the provision in section 18(a)(1A) of the Local Government Elections (Amendment) Act, 2004, which reserves one-third of the seats for women as indicated above. The third step was the enactment of the Legal Capacity of Married Persons Act, 2006, which removed the minority status of married women and repealed all laws which gave married men marital power over their wives and property. Despite the fact that the Cabinet made a decision over 16 years ago to establish a human rights commission, Lesotho has not yet established such a commission, which would work as an oversight institution to deal with issues of political participation as well. According to the Principal Secretary for Justice, Human Rights and Correctional Service, preparations are at an advanced stage to establish a human rights commission in Lesotho. The bill on the establishment of the commission was tabled before Parliament and passed the first-reading stage towards the end of 2011. In the absence of a human rights commission, all cases relating to constitutional matters have been heard by an ad hoc Constitutional Court, which is immediately disbanded after each case has been heard.

However issues around succession to the throne and chieftainship are based on customary law, which does not recognise females as legitimate claimants to these posts. The

Constitution, in section 45(1) is clear on this issue and states: 'The College of Chiefs may at any time designate, in accordance with the customary law of Lesotho, the person (or persons in order of prior right) who are entitled to succeed to the office of King. 'Succession to the office of Chief is provided for under the Chieftainship Act, 1968, which reads:

When an office of Chief becomes vacant, the firstborn or only son of the first or only marriage of the Chief succeeds to that office, and so, in descending order, that person succeeds to the office who is the firstborn or only son of the first or only marriage of a person who, but for his death or incapacity, would have succeeded to that office in accordance with the provisions of this succession. [Emphasis added]It is clear from these provisions that the senior-most legitimate sons, and not daughters, become successors to the office of King and Chief. This is because the expectation is that daughters will get married and be cut off from their lineage as they become subsumed in the affairs of their new families. In that event, they will take their chieftainship rights with them to their new families, while, customarily, the institution belongs to particular families. The wives of chiefs have an opportunity to succeed their husbands in cases where there are no male claimants to the office. Currently, the wives of the deceased Principal Chiefs of various clans, including the Phamong, Berea, Maama and 'M'amathe, for example, have succeeded their husbands and are members of the Senate. It is also common practice that senior wives of chiefs act on behalf of their minor sons until they come of age.

Equal participation

Lesotho is generally a homogeneous society and, over the centuries, intermarital arrangements across different clans have helped to prevent issues of social differentiation based on ethnicity or religion. As such, rights to participate in national politics are generally enjoyed by citizens across the nation. The national legislature, the executive, and the civil service are broadly representative of almost all geographic regions of the country. There have not been any serious issues raised by any group about under-representation. Political parties, too, draw support from across all social groups and classes, including those who claim to represent the workers. These are the Lesotho Workers Party (LWP) and the Popular Front for Democracy (PFD). The poor participate in political processes mainly through their membership of political parties, including the ruling party, and vote freely in national elections. The state provides scholarships for tertiary education, which generally benefit every qualifying student. Since the year 2000, the state provides primary education, which was made compulsory in 2010. In addition, the state currently provides pensions at the rate of

M350 (USD50 per month) to the aged from the age of 70. These are reflected in annual national budgets. In practice, women are largely able to exercise their right to participate in national politics. The government has taken deliberate affirmative action measures to appoint women to senior positions in the public service. For example, in the post-2007 elections Cabinet, there were nine women (seven Ministers and two assistant Ministers), who constituted 39% of the whole Cabinet. Following the 2012 elections, five women were appointed as Ministers and three as Deputy Ministers. This means that the Cabinet has 27% female representation, which reflects a 12% decline from the position in the previous Cabinet. However, these affirmative action policies have so far not had much impact on national politics, except that, at any one time, women are selected or appointed for public service positions for a given period, after which they go back to their previous positions in society.

Migrants and refugees

As indicated under the equal-citizenship section of this report, migrants, asylum seekers and refugees are given protection and assistance to integrate into society. Historically, Lesotho has not established special locations or camps for refugees. They have always lived among the Basotho and have attended the same schools as them. This is why, during the cross-border raids carried out by South Africa's apartheid forces in 1982 and 1985, some Basotho were killed along with members of the Pan Africanist Congress of Azania (PAC) and the African National Congress (ANC) – the two liberation movements which engaged in armed struggle against the apartheid state. The protection of these groups of people is ensured through law and practice, and there have been no cases to indicate otherwise.

With regard to political participation, these groups are legally allowed to enjoy similar rights to those of the Basotho after going through all processes and becoming citizens. No law prevents them from voting in national elections and standing as candidates. In practice, however, they have not exercised these rights, nor do they participate in community activities such as attending funerals in their communities. One classic example is the Indian community, which has been in Lesotho for decades, but has rarely sought to participate in the country's political affairs. One exception is Dr Shabir Peerbhai, a member of this group, who was appointed as Lesotho's High Commissioner to India from June 2005 to June 2011.

Conclusion and recommendations
It is clear from the above discussion that conditions for equal citizenship indeed prevail in Lesotho. No citizens are restricted from exercising their full citizenship. Lawful migrants are

generally allowed to enjoy all rights in line with the international instruments, as outlined under section B above. However, the country has not yet established a human rights commission, despite the fact that the Cabinet made a decision in this regard in 1995. Lesotho authorities should pass the bill currently before Parliament to establish a national human rights commission.

Chapter Four

Participation in the policy process

This chapter seeks to capture a sense of the depth and reach of policy debate and the extent to which citizens can participate in government and the development process. The chapter focuses on freedom of expression and the media, freedom of association, access to information, consultation and participation in policy development, and the strength of civil society.

Freedom of expression and press freedom

Lesotho has ratified both the International Covenant on Civil and Political Rights (ICCPR) and the African Charter on Human and Peoples' Rights. The former guarantees freedom of expression, and, by implication, also freedom of the press. The ICCPR states, in article 19(2):

> Everyone shall have the right to freedom of expression; this right shall include freedom to seek, receive and

impart information and ideas of all kinds, regardless of frontiers, either orally, in writing or in print, in the form of art, or through any other media of his choice.

The Constitution, 1993, complies with the above article and provides that:

Every person shall be entitled to, and (except with his own consent) shall not be hindered in his enjoyment of, freedom of expression, including freedom to hold opinions without interference, freedom to receive ideas and information without interference, freedom to communicate ideas and information without interference (whether the communication be to the public generally or to any person or class of persons) and freedom from interference with his correspondence. The African Charter on Human and Peoples' Rights, in article 9, also accords rights to receive information and the right to freedom of expression and states: (1) 'Every individual shall have the right to receive information'; and (2) 'Every individual shall have the right to express and disseminate his opinion within the law'. These provisions are expanded on by the Declaration of Principles on Freedom of Expression in Africa, 2002, under article I:

1. Freedom of expression and information, including the right to seek, receive and impart information and ideas, either orally, in writing or in print, in the form of art, or through any other form of

communication, including across frontiers, is a fundamental and inalienable human right and indispensable component of democracy.

2. Everyone shall have an equal opportunity to exercise the right to freedom of expression and to access information without discrimination.

Article II provides:

1. No one shall be subject to arbitrary interference with his or her freedom of expression.

2. Any restrictions on freedom of expression shall be provided by law, serve

3. a legitimate interest and be necessary in a democratic society.

Article VI obliges state parties to transform state- and government-controlled broadcasters into public broadcasters and to make them accountable through the legislature rather than the government, in line with the following principles:

- Public broadcasters should be governed by a board which is protected against interference, particularly of a political or economic nature;

- The editorial independence of public-service broadcasters should be guaranteed; Public broadcasters should be adequately funded in a manner that protects them from arbitrary interference with their budgets;

- Public broadcasters should strive to ensure that their transmission system covers the whole territory of the country; and

The public-service ambit of public broadcasters should be clearly defined and include an obligation to ensure that the public receive adequate, politically balanced information, articularly during election periods. These international instruments and the Constitution notwithstanding, there are serious concerns on the part of media practitioners about full enjoyment of these rights. These concerns emanate from provisions in several laws, which are regarded as placing undue restrictions on freedom of expression and on media freedom. These include, for example, the Printing and Publications Act, 1967, which is the main act regulating the print media in Lesotho. This act makes it an offence for any person to publish, distribute or redistribute any printed matter or

extract which is proven to present a danger to public safety, public morality or fundamental human rights and freedoms. The main criticism against this provision raised by some media practitioners is that it is subject to abuse, because these issues are widely open to subjective and overly broad interpretations. The Official Secrets Act, 1967, which prohibits the unauthorised obtaining or disclosure of official information, has also been criticised by some media practitioners on the grounds that it 'induces a culture of secrecy' in the public service because it 'classifies every official document as secret until the government decides otherwise'. This makes it very difficult for the media to access official information and disseminate it to the public, and also to play its watchdog role over the government. The third law is the Internal Security Act, 1984, which is similarly denounced for making it an offence for any person to utter or write any words with a subversive intention, not to disclose information that he/she knows or believes to be of material assistance in preventing any subversive activity or for securing the apprehension, prosecution or conviction of a person for an offence involving the commission, preparation or instigation of subversive activity, or publish words that might reasonably incite the commission of public violence by members of the public. This act is regarded as 'turning people into informers for the authorities even on the basis of suspicions about the conduct of others'. The argument here is that journalists are most likely to come across information considered to be subversive in their daily duties and thus become vulnerable to the law, which requires them to become informers to the authorities. This would compromise their independence and freedom to gather information, as the public would become suspicious of them and undermine their proper role in society. This law would also undermine the confidentiality of sources of information as an internationally recognised principle of journalism, and lead to self-censorship by the media. In practice, citizens of Lesotho enjoy their rights to freedom of association and freedom of the media to a large degree, but there are some exceptions. In the words of one respondent, 'prior to, during and post elections you expect conflicts and often you find journalists getting caught in these conflicts and then suffer[ing] the wrath of the government. The government uses the Internal Security Act, 1984, where journalists are accused of being seditious. 'The Constitution and other laws protect freedom of the media (including broadcast, print and 'new' media).

There are, however, some restrictions on the media imposed by outdated laws such as the Abdications and Proclamation Act of 1912, the Sedition and Proclamation Act, 1967, and the Internal Security Act, 1984, which the government invokes to suppress the media from time to time. Media practitioners have for a long time fought for their rights, but their views are not heard by the government. There are no restrictions regarding registration of media houses. As long as they have financial resources, they are free to register their businesses. The only restriction is that airwave frequencies allocated by the state are not always available. But media houses can install their own transmitters if they can afford it. Those opposing government policy do not generally have equitable access to the state media, which has wider coverage than privately owned media. These include state-owned Radio Lesotho and Television Lesotho. The opposition is only allowed limited access to state media during election campaigns, when there is a mandatory slot allocated to them by the elections management body. This is in line with the National Assembly Electoral Act, 2011, and also with the SADC Principles and Guidelines Governing Democratic Elections, which advocates for equal opportunity for political parties to access state-owned media. But there are no laws proscribing specific individuals from having access to state media to air their views. Similarly, there are no laws governing the professional conduct of journalists or standards of news reporting in the broadcast media during election time or at any other time.

The reporting by private media is impartial in practice. However, the government uses the state-owned and state-controlled media to project its propaganda and positions, and it is not impartial. Government officials and ruling-party officials also have preferential access to the state media. The state media comprise the Lesotho Today/Lentsoe la Basotho newspaper, the

Lesotho News Agency, Lesotho Television, Radio Lesotho and Ultimate FM. The state media collectively enjoy much wider coverage than all non-state media combined. The private media therefore try to provide a platform for opposition parties, but they also provide the government with a platform; hence the non-state media are generally much more impartial in their coverage of elections. In practice, in the community and in general life, there is widespread and uncensored debate about political issues. People also talk freely and in an uncensored way in the private media (print and radio), but the same cannot be said about state media, where editorial content as well as people who call into radio talk shows are censored.

Access to information

Citizens do not have a legal right of access to government information. The government makes it impossible for the media to obtain official information without the blessing of principal secretaries, who are the heads of different government ministries. Thus, in practice, there is no effective access to such information. There is also no freedom of information law in Lesotho. The media fraternity has been fighting for over 11 years for enactment of the Access and Receipt of Information Bill, 2000, passed by Parliament, but without success. The government has not passed this into law for unclear reasons.

There have been various efforts by MISA-Lesotho to push for access to official government information. These include a mini-study covering eight public institutions, intended to assess the extent to which government information is easily accessible. MISA–Lesotho published the results of this effort in a bid to sensitise society, as well as the government, on the issue of public access to information. In eight written requests for information, only three responses were received to the letters issued by MISA–Lesotho requesting what is otherwise public information. Many of the ministries of government performed poorly in this exercise. The Ministry of Home Affairs and Public Safety was found to be the most secretive ministry in Lesotho, while a parastatal, the Lesotho Communications Authority, was found to be the most open institution. The Ministry of Health and Social Welfare is quoted as having said in its response, among other things: 'As already known, Government ministries cannot release any information in the respective ministries without the principal secretaries' consent [...]. The information could not be released without valid reason as to what it is needed for. 'Since there is no legal right of access to official information, official budgetary and expenditure information also remains hidden. On this point, Matjama had this to say:

No, no. If you look at, I don't know if I may call it a tract, but from 2003 to 2008 there was no audit. If you ask there will be no answer but if you want to access the records you won't have access to such records. There have been budgetary variations even from that time when audits were not made; up to now there are still variations. People have no access to the information about these variations and all transactions that were made. Now there was a businessman who was lent M15 million and if you ask how that was recorded in government accounts you won't get an answer. There are also no effective or fair processes (including appeals) to determine when government can claim that certain information is confidential.

Freedom of association

The Constitution, 1993, recognises freedom of association and expressly states that: Every person shall be entitled to, and (except with his own consent) shall not be hindered in his enjoyment of freedom to associate freely with other persons for ideological, religious, political, economic, labour, social, cultural, recreational and similar purposes. People are allowed to register their different associations for whatever lawful purposes under the Societies Act, 1967. Members of civil society organisations agree that the right to organise in order to participate in public-policy debates is highly recognised in Lesotho, and this right is protected by both the Constitution and other subordinate laws. The government does not interfere with the human right to participate as provided for in law. In practice, however, the country still has a long way to go. In the area of labour relations, there are stringent conditions under which recognition agreements between employers and employees can be signed. In the textile industry, total membership of a trade union has to be at least 50+1% of the total workforce before the union can be legally recognised. This requirement is too stringent and leaves the workers literally without rights before they reach this number. 97 With regard to funding, there are no specific requirements obstructing the establishment of civic groups. Registration deposits are not exorbitant and are within reach of most aspiring organisations.

Although civil society in Lesotho was described as playing an ambivalent role in the democratisation process in Lesotho, things seem to have changed recently, and the role of civil society in politics seems to be progressing in the direction of what one can expect in a democratising system. Consequently, the government does not harass civil society organisations openly or physically when they are critical of it. Nevertheless, Matjama believes that the new Public Processions and Meetings Act, 2010, curtails freedom of association. In one incident, the Ministry of Local Government ordered a District Secretary to deny officials from two NGOs, the Transformation Resource Centre (TRC) and Development for Peace Education (DPE), access to local councillors in some areas that the two organisations worked in. These two organisations had been holding workshops for newly elected councillors, and the government argued that it first had to inaugurate these councillors before they could carry out any public duties. The two organisations, however, were of the view that the government was taking too long to have the councillors inaugurated.

Consultation and participation in policy development

Parliament has established Social Cluster Portfolio Committees that should gather the views of the public about new and amended legislation, but the process is hardly effective. There are no other permanent or effective institutions with the mandate to facilitate consultation on policy development, despite the Labour Code providing for the establishment of structures involving government, industry and labour. As such, when policies and laws are formulated, public consultation takes place merely on the basis of willingness on the part of the government. 101 When civil society organisations (CSOs) want the opportunity to make an input in public policies, they have to struggle very hard to achieve this, because public consultation is not common in Lesotho. On issues such as the national budget, the process is highly elitist. Citizens merely become recipients of state-developed policies without making any input in their formulation. The budget is mainly informed and developed by departments of government. CSOs are allowed to comment on the budget after it has been presented to Parliament, and budget documents are only presented to the public after presentation in Parliament. Consequently, one of the CSOs, the DPE has taken it upon itself to sensitise citizens about important policies through the holding of peoples' parliaments and tribunals.

These forums do have some influence on the policy priorities of the government in certain instances. In one case, a year after participants in the peoples' parliament from Hloahloeng and Koebunyane had indicated their priority needs as a bridge over the Senqu River and a signal for mobile phones, the government provided the requisite infrastructure for mobile phones, and these have become functional in the areas concerned. It also built a bridge and this was officially opened in December 2010. However, in the few cases where Social Cluster Portfolio Committees have ascertained the public's views, Parliament has usually disregarded these and passed the laws in question unchanged, conduct which is obviously contrary to the general public interest. One such case is the Land Act Bill, 2011, and the National University of Lesotho (NUL) Amendment Bill, 2011. The two bills were roundly condemned by the public but were passed by Parliament. Government departmental planning schedules are almost non-existent, and, where they exist, such schedules are not open to the general public. There are no effective systems for public consultation in cases where the government is planning major development projects that will have an impact on large numbers of people.

Whenever such projects have been undertaken, individual organisations such as the Lesotho Highlands Development Authority (LHDA) have devised their own consultation systems, which are not necessarily guided by any national framework. However, government strategies to reduce poverty and achieve the Millennium Development Goals (MDGs) were indeed developed in a consultative way. Organisations such as the TRC and others were part of the training workshop facilitated by the Ministry of Development Planning to formulate the country's Poverty Reduction Strategy Paper (PRSP). A Technical Working Group composed of the LCN and Principal Secretaries and Directors of government ministries and departments formulated the PRSP document, which has been hailed by the international community as the outcome of a highly consultative process. The consultation process took place across the country and included such groups as NGOs, chiefs and the general public. However, implementation of the MDGs was a closed process, in that it was a government project without any involvement on the part of civil society. Its implementation has been haphazard and government does not have clear, specific plans, reflected in the annual national budget, for the achievement of the MDGs. There is also no link between what the government and civil society are doing towards achievement of these MDGs.

The strength of civil society

There are several CSOs whose mandate includes lobbying and advocacy activities. These are organised under the LCN through different commissions: agriculture; natural resources; justice; democracy and human rights; disaster and humanitarian relief; and health and social development. The membership of these organisations overlaps across these commissions, such that one organisation appears under more than one commission. The organisations are found throughout the country, both in the rural and urban areas. The strength of civil society in Lesotho lies in its ability to interact easily with people at the lowest grassroots levels. It is further rendered strong by its ability to raise critical issues concerning the government. Besides, CSOs have to date been politically impartial, despite an assumption by some in government that they align themselves with certain opposition political parties. Civil society is therefore independent and quite credible.

Despite these notable strengths, civil society in Lesotho has weaknesses. The main weakness is lack of resources, particularly human resources. Consequently, civil society is no longer able to fight as hard as it used to when critical issues arise. Whenever outstanding individuals emerge within CSOs, they are snatched up by the government and public institutions that offer better remuneration. Furthermore, CSOs have a weakness in relation to the programmes they run. Most of these organisations are involved with too many issues and aspects of the themes they focus on and find it difficult to specialise. As a result, they are not as efficient as they could otherwise be..

Conclusion and recommendations

Public participation in the policy process in Lesotho remains very poor. To ensure public participation in policy and law-making, Parliament has established various Portfolio Committees, which are yet to become effective. The general process of policy-making is still the preserve of government bureaucracy, with no or little input from citizens and their organisations outside government. In recent years, the government has been inviting citizens to discuss the national budget after it has been tabled in Parliament, but not during its preparation. Although the Basotho are generally free to express themselves about any issues of national importance during interpersonal and wider social discourse, there are still legal hurdles that curtail the operations of a free media. The country continues to retain outdated laws, which make it difficult for media practitioners to do their work. Those opposing the government generally do not have access to state-owned media. There is no law guaranteeing citizens access to information held by government. In 2010, the government pushed a controversial Public Processions and Meetings Act through Parliament, which various groups and organisations in society regard as repressive. Further, Lesotho does not have a human rights commission.

In the light of the above issues, the following recommendations are made:

1. Parliament should do more to open itself to adequate public participation through its Portfolio Committees, including the use of public hearings and written submissions on bills placed before it;

2. It should have a regularly updated website on which all pending legislation, notices of the dates and places of hearings, notices of the dates and deadlines for submissions, and the addresses to which submissions have to be sent, should be posted;

3. The government should invite and assist citizens to make an input during national budget preparation in order to ensure that the budget reflects the needs of the people; The government should review all laws related to the

media and repeal those which are outdated and inhibit media freedom;

4. It should also transform the state-owned broadcaster into an editorially independent public broadcaster;

5. The government should pass into law the Access and Receipt of Information Bill, 2000, to ensure that citizens have access to official information and to effect transparency in government;

6. The government should revisit the Public Processions and Meetings Act, 2010, with a view to ensuring that citizens enjoy their constitutional right to freedom of association; and Parliament should pass the Human. Rights Commission Bill to facilitate the establishment of such a commission

Chapter Five

Elections

Since the return of Lesotho to multi-party politics in 1993, the country has held five rounds of elections (1993, 1998, 2002, 2007 and 2012). Despite the fact that the process of holding elections has not been smooth, with the losers contesting the outcome, these elections have been conducted within the legal framework and in line with international, African and regional treaties and standards. Using the data generated through personal interviews with purposively selected respondents,[113] this chapter focuses on the following issues: the legal and institutional framework of elections, electoral administration, voter registration, voter education and participation, the electoral system, electoral malpractice, election observation, and validity of results.

A. Legal and institutional framework

The Constitution, 1993, provides that 'Parliament shall continue for five years from the date when the two Houses of Parliament first meet after any dissolution',and this effectively means that the election timetable is fixed for at least five years, and that the country must hold elections within this time. The country has adhered to relevant international standards such as articles 4 and 5 of the Treaty of the Southern African Development Community (SADC), the SADC Protocol on Defence, Politics and Security Co-operation, as well as the SADC's Principles and Guidelines for Conducting Democratic Elections. Lesotho has been abiding by these commitments since the 1993 transitional elections. It has further introduced a local-government system, and, in this regard, held two local elections (2005 and 2011). All citizens of Lesotho are legally allowed to register and vote in all elections.

Electoral administration

Elections in Lesotho are managed by the Independent Electoral Commission (IEC) established in 1997. The Commission is headed by three commissioners, with one serving as chairperson. The commissioners are appointed through an inclusive process that involves all political parties registered with the Commission. Political parties nominate five candidates, in the case where all three seats on the Commission are to be filled, and nominate three candidates when only one post is to be filled.

The names of the nominees, accompanied by their curriculum vitae, are then handed to the Council of State in order of preference, which, in turn, submits them to the King along with the Council's recommendations and order of preference. The King makes the final appointments. Like the political parties that make the nominations, the Council of State does not conduct interviews with the nominees. Instead, the selection is made on the basis of the nominees' curriculum vitae. It is also worth noting, some of the respondents emphasised, 'that the order of preference made by the political parties is in no way binding on the Council of State'. This reality gives the ruling party an unfair advantage over the opposition, in that the Council of State is mostly composed of the appointees of the King acting on the binding advice of the Prime Minister, who is the leader of the ruling party. Such members, in the view of one respondent 'will always ensure the candidate favoured by the ruling party is given the post'. The rest of the Commission's staff consist of civil servants recruited and paid by the public service. Some respondents have indicated that efforts are being made to change the situation and to make the staff full-time employees of the Commission.

There were mixed feelings among the respondents about the impartiality and effectiveness of the IEC. Concerning impartiality, most respondents felt the Commission was impartial. However, one respondent complained it was not impartial and, according to him, it usually gives preferential treatment to the ruling party. With regard to effectiveness, there was a consensus among the respondents that the Commission is not very effective. Examples of the ineffectiveness of the Commission were drawn from the problems encountered in the administration of the local-government elections held in October 2011. These elections, according to the respondents, were characterised by various problems, including faulty voter lists, the late opening of voting stations, the non-arrival of voting material (leading to postponement of voting to the next day in some cases), and delays in announcing the results.

The ineffectiveness of the IEC was mostly attributed by the respondents to structural problems and lack of capacity. One respondent pointed out an example of weakness in the structure of the IEC. The respondent complained that, despite the Director of Elections being such a vital post in the administration of elections, the position has been occupied by an acting person since the substantive director went on retirement over two years ago. The competence of IEC personnel was generally doubted by some of the respondents. Some respondents named crucial positions within the Commission which, in their view, were occupied by incompetent

staff. One such position is that of the officer responsible for party registration. This position is allegedly occupied by a former head of security at the Commission. The officer, according to one respondent, 'has not been trained for the new job and remains completely incompetent'.

While the respondents generally agreed that the IEC is independent in terms of law, they gave different views about its independence in practice. This difference of opinion seemed to derive from membership of the respondents' parties. All the respondents from the opposition parties argued that the IEC is not independent. They generally agreed that it serves mainly to 'promote' the interests of the ruling party. This claim was, however, refuted by respondents from the ruling party, who claimed that the Commission treated their party like all other parties. With regard to IEC funding, all the respondents agreed that the Commission is adequately funded. They noted that the Ministry of Finance and Planning is always prepared to provide even contingency budgets for the Commission whenever the need arises. Furthermore, the respondents acknowledged the role played by donors and international institutions like the

United Nations Development Programme (UNDP) in closing whatever financial gaps appeared in the IEC's budget.

Voter registration, education and participation

Lesotho uses a continuous voter registration system. All the respondents were of the view that, although the law requires it to do so, the IEC has failed to regularly update the voters' register and that the register remains unreliable. In support of this claim, the respondents cited the contents of the report titled 'The state of the voters' roll as at July 2011'. This is a report compiled by elections expert, Roberts Johnson. According to this report, 'as at July 2011 Lesotho's voters' roll was inflated by over 100 000 voters because the IEC had failed to clean the register regularly'. The revelation was made following the company's audit of the lists prior to local-government elections held in October 2011. Some respondents further noted that, owing to its unreliable registration technology, the IEC had failed dismally to register new voters, particularly the youth. The respondents did, however, acknowledge that efforts were being made by the Commission to remedy this situation. These include the purchasing of about 600 portable machines that IEC officials can carry with them in order to register new voters at public gatherings such as political- party rallies. According to one respondent, about 300 of these machines were scheduled to be delivered by suppliers to the Commission before the end of 2011. The machines were, however, not delivered because of the limited time available to train staff on how to use them for the 2012 elections.

Although they regard the voters' register as unreliable, the respondents generally agreed that the register does not provide opportunities for 'ghost voting' or similar electoral fraud. This is guarded against by the complex voting process in the country. The process involves not only IEC personnel, but law-enforcement officers (the police) and, most importantly, agents of political parties. All of these are involved in all stages of voting from identification of each and every voter, balancing the number of votes against the voters' register, counting of votes to announcement of results at the polling stations.

All the respondents were of the view that all social groups were well represented in the voters' register. Furthermore, all people, including prisoners, vote in Lesotho's elections. Only citizens who have committed electoral offences and prisoners on death row are legally not allowed to vote. These are, however, very rare occurrences.

The country normally conducts advance voting for electoral staff and other citizens who are on duty on polling day so that they are able to exercise their right to vote. However, advance voting was not conducted prior to the October 2011 local-government elections. This means that the above stated categories were impliedly denied their right to participate in the elections. The respondents generally showed concern regarding these developments and called for this anomaly to be corrected in the 2012 general elections. Although voters who are resident outside the country are legally allowed to vote, in practice they fail to do so unless they are in the country on polling day. Arrangements are normally made to facilitate voting on site for staff of the country's embassies. This arrangement is however limited to embassy staff and does not include other groups such as migrant workers and students studying at institutions outside Lesotho. This once again means that these people are impliedly disenfranchised.

There are also no official arrangements to ensure that the sick and disabled vote in Lesotho's elections. This is different from countries like South Africa, one respondent complained, where administrative electoral institutions normally make an effort to visit sick voters in hospitals. In Lesotho, the respondents generally agreed, it remains the responsibility of the political parties to help take their sick and disabled members to the polling stations. Such voters are usually given special preference, such as skipping the queues at polling stations.

Provision of voter education remains a challenge in Lesotho. This has in the past remained the responsibility of the IEC. The Commission has, however, proved to lack the capacity to adequately deliver this important task. In an effort to remedy this deficiency, the Commission has outsourced the task to local, non-governmental organisations. Prior to the October 2011 local-government elections, the IEC signed an agreement with the Lesotho Council of Non-Governmental Organisations (LCN), allowing the latter to provide voter education for voters. However, the process was delayed due to logistical reasons, but the involvement of the LCN in voter education is hailed as a positive step by all respondents from stakeholders in Lesotho's elections. Apart from the engagement of the LCN, the IEC has also trained youth members of registered political parties in proper voting procedures. These members, in turn, help train their own party members. This has also been well received by the political parties.

Electoral system

As indicated in chapter 1 of this report, Lesotho uses the Mixed Member Proportional (MMP) electoral system in which the First-Past-The-Post (FPTP) system is used to elect 80 constituency-based MPs alongside 40 others elected under the PR party-list system. This system has gone a long way in making Parliament more inclusive and representative, thus leading to political stability in the country. The system allocates parliamentary seats based on an agreed formula (total votes/total seats = quota; total party votes/quota = party seats), which is applied in several stages until all seats have been allocated. Since its adoption, ten parties secured parliamentary seats in the 2002 election and 12 parties in the 2007 and 2012 elections.

Electoral malpractice

Concerning mechanisms for ensuring freeness and fairness in political campaigns, all the respondents agreed that there are challenges. The respondents further agreed that there is a binding Code of Conduct that all participating political parties and independent candidates are subject to. 117 This Code of Conduct gives the IEC powers to discipline, and even to take to court, individuals and political parties that are deemed to be in breach of it. The objective of the Code is to promote conditions conducive to conducting free and fair elections within a tolerant and democratic environment in which political parties can carry out their activities without fear, coercion, intimidation, and reprisals. 118 Through this Code, the IEC has the legal power to ensure that campaigns are free and fair. However, all respondents, including those from government, agreed that, because of its access to state resources, the ruling party has an advantage over its competitors in this regard. This is because members of the opposition hardly have the resources to fund their political campaigns. There is no strong private sector that could help to solve the problem either. The respondents did, however, note that, starting in 2012, the IEC plans to introduce campaign funding for political parties contesting elections. This funding of parties has been hailed by the respondents as a positive effort by the IEC.

The law in Lesotho allows incumbent Ministers unrestricted use of state vehicles. While one respondent from the ruling party was of the view that the IEC has no control over this imbalance, as it is allegedly a norm all over the world, respondents from the opposition parties felt it was within the legal right of the IEC to stop the practice. Respondents, particularly from the opposition parties, complained that the IEC has, in the past, failed dismally to sanction ruling- party members for violating the electoral Code of Conduct. Two examples were given in support of this assertion. The first relates to a case in which computers were allegedly distributed to schools within the Machache constituency by government officials, just days prior to the polling day for the 2007 general election. In the same constituency, the police confiscated a government mini-bus that was allegedly being used to transport supporters of the ruling party to the polling stations. Five years after the incident, some respondents noted, the mini-bus remains at the police station and the IEC has never taken any measures against the ruling party or its candidate. Another example relates to allegations of food aid being strategically distributed to constituencies a few days before the October 2011 local-government elections.

Respondents also raised concerns about the increasingly discriminatory use of public resources by ordinary ruling-party members for their campaigns. They complained that there is an emerging trend where some of the principal secretaries, though not legally allowed to do so like incumbent Ministers, are openly using public resources to campaign for the ruling party's candidacy in their respective constituencies. Apart from vehicles, respondents from the opposition parties complained that the ruling party has unlimited access to the state media throughout the year, while their parties are only allowed a few brief slots – paid for by the IEC – on national radio and television, barely about a month before elections.

The respondents were in general agreement that the ruling party has never used existing electoral laws, created new ones, or amended the Constitution to prevent registration of parties or candidates that are likely to form a significant challenge to it. Respondents from the opposition parties however claimed that the ruling party does, on occasion, covertly and overtly abuse the law to hinder legitimate activities of the opposition parties. In support of their claim, respondents from the opposition cited certain examples. One respondent, a former MP, noted that the ruling party abused the law by calling the army to quell a sit-in in Parliament in 2007. This, according to the respondent, was contrary to parliamentary regulations, as the call was not made by the Speaker from the chair, but through the sergeant at arms. Respondents also claimed that the ruling party has, through the police, obscured the marches of the opposition from the public eye by imposing awkward and isolated routes for such marches. The claim was denied by the respondent from the ruling party.

Despite all the challenges facing the electoral process in Lesotho, the country has never experienced violence during elections. For instance, the outbreaks of violence in 1998 took place in September, four months after the elections, while that of 2007 emanated from disputes over the allocation of parliamentary seats after the elections. This lack of violence was explained by some respondents as not necessarily resulting from any effective action by either the IEC or the government, but was attributable to the homogeneous nature of Basotho society. Normally, the state deploys only one police officer per polling station, a number hardly adequate to quell violence if it erupted.

Election observation

Since Lesotho's return to multi-party politics in 1993, all parliamentary elections have been observed by international and local observers, including the Commonwealth, the SADC, and local observers from civil society organisations. The process of election observation is provided for in the National Assembly Electoral Act, 2011, and both local and international observers are allowed to observe various stages of elections in Lesotho. The international observers arrive about a week before elections and leave about six days after the poll. Thus far, observers have generally declared elections to be a reflection of the will of the voters. In the 2007 parliamentary elections, for example, one mission concluded that:

Notwithstanding the challenges created by a snap election, the National Assembly elections in Lesotho held on the 17 February 2007 were conducted in a manner and environment that, to a large extent, allowed the Basotho people to express their will freely. 121Similarly, the Commonwealth Observer Mission found that the 2007 elections were credible and allowed the Basotho to freely express their will. 122 The same mission had observed previous elections and had made several recommendations to ensure improvement in the conduct of future elections. It found, however, that some of its earlier recommendations following the 2002 elections had not been implemented by the Lesotho authorities. It had recommended, among other things, that the ruling party should desist from using government resources during the campaigning period, that constituency and party ballots should be provided simultaneously to speed up the voting process, and that constituencies should communicate their results directly to the headquarters rather than through the district office to in order to avoid delays and suspicions of vote-rigging. 123 In the recent 2012 polls, too, both domestic and international observers declared the electoral process as having been free, fair and credible, despite some concerns raised by various stakeholders. The country's civil society organisations have also been involved in election observation at the invitation of the IEC. However, the observation was effective only for the 2007 national elections, while the same cannot be said about the 2011 local-government elections. The former election had a large number of observers, whereas the latter was observed by a few observers only and, by implication, only in a few areas of the country. Most of the local observers were funded by the LCN. In the 2007 elections, the observer teams were deployed well before polling day and remained until after the announcement of the results. However, this was not the case with the 2011 local-government elections.

The recommendations made by local and international observers were generally similar and were mainly centred on the incompetence of the IEC. The observers recommended that the competence of the polling staff and that of voters in general be improved. Specifically with regard to voters' competence, the recommendation has consistently been that the IEC outsource voter education to civil society organisations. This recommendation was adopted and voter education was conducted by the LCN prior to the local-government elections. The IEC called for an expression of interest from the NGOs for conducting voter education for the 2012 general elections and the LCN conducted this exercise. Furthermore, the IEC trained the youth leagues of political parties in voting procedures. This approach has the potential positive result of better-informed youth leagues that do not have misconceptions about the electoral process.

Validity of results

Other than in 1993 and 1998, election results have generally been accepted as a genuine reflection of the popular will. There are effective and equitable processes of announcing the results. The rule dictates that election results for different polling stations be announced at such stations immediately after counting has been completed and the figures have been signed for by all the electoral staff and contesting parties' agents. The totals from different polling stations are then taken to the central office where they are computed to produce overall figures for councils and constituencies during local council and general elections respectively. From the constituencies, these results are then taken to the national central point where overall national scores are announced. The rules for announcing results have generally been observed to the letter in the past.

Adjudication of electoral disputes is still a problem. The use of the courts as a mechanism for resolving electoral disputes is not ideal. 126 A clear example is the infamous MFP case on the allocation of parliamentary seats after the 2007 elections. Despite being instituted in 2007, this case only came to an end in 2009. The case was decided by the High Court, not on its substantive merits, but on technicalities, including the fact that the MFP did not have locus standi and that the court did not have jurisdiction over the case.

Conclusion and recommendations

Elections in Lesotho have been the main cause of conflict since independence. The political leadership of the country has taken important steps to overcome many challenges relating to the manner in which elections are managed, including establishing the IEC to manage parliamentary and local elections. The IEC is working very closely with all stakeholders in all its activities. This is a positive development which has huge potential for improving the image of the Commission and for reducing problems related to the management of elections. However, the Commission has not been able to maintain a clean and credible voters' register. The current register still includes names of deceased persons, and new voters are not adequately registered, even when they attempt to register, because of unreliable registration systems. The Commission still draws staff from the public service, which is regarded by the opposition as incompetent.

Key recommendations on the management of elections include the following:

- The IEC should thoroughly review and clean up the voters' roll to ensure the credibility of elections in Lesotho;
- Political elites should learn to resolve election-related disputes through negotiations and only revert to the courts of law as a final resort;
- The IEC should develop its own human resource capacity rather than relying on the government for staff;
- The IEC should keep up the good work of working closely with politicians to promote transparency in its work; and
- Parliament should pass a law establishing an autonomous body specifically responsible for registration of political

parties. In the interim, one of the commissioners of the IEC

- should be tasked to deal with this issue.

Chapter Six

Political parties

This chapter describes and analyses the constitutional and legal framework within which political parties in Lesotho exist and work as key institutions providing citizens with the opportunity to participate in politics. It also assesses the extent to which laws regulating political parties in Lesotho comply with international instruments to which the country has committed itself. It further analyses the organisation and membership of political parties, the extent of internal democracy within parties and of participation of members in policy development, funding of political parties, and the strength of the multi-party system in Lesotho.

Constitutional and legal framework for political parties

The Constitution, in section 1(1), provides that 'Lesotho shall be a sovereign democratic Kingdom' which is based on the enjoyment of fundamental human rights. These human rights are entrenched in the Constitution under chapter II, including freedom of association. Section 16 expressly states:

1. Every person shall be entitled to, and (except with his own consent) shall not be hindered in his enjoyment of freedom to associate freely with other persons for ideological, religious, political, economic, labour, social, cultural, recreational and similar purposes.

There are some provisos, however, namely that:

2. Nothing contained in or done under the authority of any law shall be held to be inconsistent with or in contravention of any law to the extent that the law in question makes provision –

(a) in the interests of defence, public safety, public order, public morality or public health;

(b) for the purpose of protecting the rights and freedoms of other persons; or

(c) for the purpose of imposing restrictions upon public officers.

In line with these constitutional provisions for freedom of association, citizens of Lesotho are legally allowed to establish political parties under two legal instruments. The first is the Societies Act, 1966, under which political parties are registered in the same way as any other society in the country. More specifically, political parties have to comply with the following provisions at the Law Office of the Registrar-General:

- Pay a general registration fee of M100 (USD14. 28);Pay a fee of M40 (USD5. 71) to register and reserve the name of the party; Pay an annual renewal fee of M40 (USD5. 71);

- Provide the name and address of the party;

- Provide copies of the party's constitution, rules and code of conduct; and Provide a list of the party's office bearers.

As soon as any political party submits its application and complies with the above requirements, it is duly registered. These requirements are extremely liberal and not onerous in the least. The Registrar-General is empowered to de-register any political party if it fails to pay its registration fee or if it voluntarily dissolves itself. However, no political party has been de-registered, even though many of them have not been paying their annual renewal fees to the Registrar-General. Having duly registered with the Law Office, political parties are also required to register, for purposes of contesting elections, with the Independent Electoral Commission (IEC) in terms of the National Assembly Electoral Act, 2011. This act is a very comprehensive legal instrument covering almost all aspects of elections as a means of ensuring political participation in Lesotho. Registration of political parties is provided for under chapter 3, section 23, of this act, which section states that 'a political party shall not contest an election or sponsor a candidate for election unless it is registered with the Commission in terms of section 24'. Section 24 spells out the requirements that political parties must meet before they can be registered. Subsection 1 of this section reads:

A political party may apply for registration with the Commission if:

(a) it is a party registered under the Societies Act, 1966;

(b) its membership is voluntary and open to all citizens of Lesotho without discrimination on the grounds of race, colour, gender, language, religion, nationality or social origin, property, birth or other status;

(c) it has adopted a name and symbol that does not conflict with the limitations contained in section 33;

(d) it has adopted a party constitution that does not conflict with subsection (2);

(e) it has adopted a constitution that meets the requirements of subsection (3); and

(f) it has a paid-up membership of at least 500 electors [voters].

The Commission is empowered to verify the paid-up membership of political parties under subsection (2). This reads as follows:

The Commission shall verify the paid-up membership of a political party intending to register with it by checking:

(a) a register for membership of the political party or a membership card; and

(b) the political party membership register.

The Commission is also given powers to prohibit re-registration of political parties for five years if they have furnished false information upon registration. The IEC is also empowered to de-register political parties if:

- it is satisfied that a political party no longer exists;
- it has been notified by a party that it has dissolved or intends to dissolve;
- its membership is not voluntary and is not open to all citizens of Lesotho without discrimination on the grounds of race, colour, sex, language, religion, national or social origin, property, birth or status;
- by its constitution or policy its sole intention is to advocate or exclusively promote the interests of any

religious belief or group, a specific area or part of the Kingdom of Lesotho, or any ethnic or racial group;

- its name, symbol, etc., portrays the propagation of, or incitement to, violence or hatred; and

- it is likely to cause offence to members of the public or is such that the electoral system

- would be likely to be brought into disrepute.

The application for registration has to be submitted by the president, chairperson or secretary general of the party in the prescribed form and must be accompanied by the following:

- a copy of the party's constitution indicating its name, its abbreviated name, and its distinguishing symbol;

- the prescribed application fee;

- a declaration on a prescribed form signed by not less than 500 paid-up members whose names appear on the register;

- particulars of all assets and liabilities and all bank accounts of the party; a statement from the bank indicating the party's bank account; and any other prescribed documents.

When all these requirements have been met by the registering party, the Commission has the power to verify all the information contained in the submitted documents and, if it is satisfied therewith, the Director of Elections issues the party with a registration certificate in the prescribed form and publishes the particulars of such registration in the Government Gazette in accordance with electoral law. 132 The Commission is obliged to maintain a register of political parties and to retain copies of all documents submitted to it, and relevant to registration, for purposes of public inspection. 133While the Commission can de-register political parties as outlined above, political parties also have the right to appeal against any decision of the Commission to the High Court. 134These two legal instruments form the legal framework for registration and for participation of political parties in election. They are fairly compliant with important international instruments on democracy and on freedom of association and assembly, including the NEPAD Declaration on Democracy, Political, Economic and Corporate Governance, which the Kingdom of Lesotho has ratified. Among other things, the Declaration commits member states to upholding:

individual and collective freedoms, including the right to form and join political parties and trade unions, in conformity with the constitution; the inalienable right of the individual to participate by means of free, credible and democratic political processes in periodically electing their leaders for a fixed term of office. The Solemn Declaration on the Conference on Security,

Stability, Development and Cooperation in Africa (CSSDCA) states that 'democracy, good governance, respect for human and peoples' rights and adherence to the rule of law are prerequisites for the security, stability and development of the continent'. As can be seen from the above, the electoral laws in Lesotho are liberal and do not restrict political parties, and the requirements for registration of political parties do not prevent or obstruct freedom of association or legitimate participation. Consequently, despite its small population relative to other countries on the continent, Lesotho, with a population of 1.8 million people, has seen a proliferation of political parties since the transitional elections of 1993. At the time of writing this report (July 2012), at least 23 political parties were registered with the IEC, with more likely to register before the legislative elections in 2012.

The two legal instruments governing elections are administered by separate state organs, that is, the Law Office in the case of the Societies Act, 1966, and the IEC in the case of the National Assembly Electoral Act, 2011. While the latter act advocates for democratic, non-discriminatory and universal political parties in Lesotho, it will be seen in subsequent chapters of this report that, in daily practices, many parties are more in breach of these ideals than in conformity with the law. Many of the parties fail to meet all the legal requirements, especially in relation to provision of their physical addresses, the holding of democratic leadership elections, payment of annual renewal fees to the IEC, and other administrative provisions. In respect of this state of affairs, the IEC has implemented a recommendation by the Commonwealth Expert Team that 'registration of political parties should be examined and regulated to ensure that 500 people who seek to register a party are on the electoral list'. The IEC has embarked on a process of strictly enforcing the National Assembly Electoral Act, 2011, by ensuring that all parties registered with it meet all the stipulated requirements. Consequently, it has deregistered 12 political parties which did not meet all the legal requirements, including the requirement that political parties must have operational offices, membership registers and national executive committees..

Party organisation and membership

Despite minor variations, Lesotho's political parties include organisational structures with roots at the lowest level of society. The highest decision-making body for all parties is the annual national conference, which elects the respective national executive committees. Some parties have special conferences, which operate as extraordinary mechanisms to deal with urgent matters that cannot wait for the sitting of an annual national conference. In most of these parties, the hierarchical structure consists of the executive committees, followed by the constituency committees, branch committees and sub-branch committees (in the case of those with their origins in the Basutoland Congress Party [BCP]). In the case of the parties which are splinter groups from the Basotho National Party (BNP), the hierarchical structure usually includes the national executive committee, followed by constituency, ward and village committees. The congress parties (those derived from the BCP) also have provincial structures or committees which are based in the Republic of South Africa. This is because, historically, most Basotho men worked in South African mines and the BCP had a large following among these men. Despite their differences, constitutions of the parties clearly espouse participation in the structures of the parties in all their activities.

Internal democracy and participation in policy development

The literature on political parties in Lesotho points to a lack of internal democracy within parties. Almost all the main political parties in Lesotho have for a long time been embroiled in internal squabbles over power and senior party positions. As a consequence of internal conflicts, many of these parties have now developed what may be described as a 'culture of splitting' each time that the country approaches legislative elections. This trend started at the inception of the multi-party system when the two original main parties (the BNP and the Marematlou Freedom Party [MFP]) broke away from the BCP prior to independence. The trend became more pervasive after the 1993 transitional elections and still continues to date. After each election, Lesotho's opposition parties have never accepted the results, leading to conflicts between winners and losers. In the run-up to the 2012 elections, there were serious tensions between the two factions of the then ruling Lesotho Congress for Democracy (LCD) (locally known as Litima-mollo and Lija-mollo) or, simply translated, 'fire extinguishers and fire eaters' respectively. This conflict led to the Prime Minister dismissing, from the Cabinet, Mr Mothejoa Metsing, the Minister of Communications, Science and Technology, the Secretary-General of the LCD, Mr Motloheloa Phooko, who was the Minister in the Prime Minister's Office, Mr Khotso Matla, Assistant Minister in the Ministry of Trade and Industry, Cooperatives and Marketing and also the Publicity Secretary of the LCD. The main opposition, the All Basotho Convention (ABC), has also experienced in-fighting, which has led to some of its MPs crossing the floor to the ruling LCD. The latest of these has been Mr Motumi Ralejoe of the Lithabaneng constituency.

Ordinary members of political parties in Lesotho have little or no input in the development of policy by their respective parties.

The exercise remains the responsibility of the leaders and their national executive committees (NECs). But even the leaders and their NECs, according to Matlosa and Sello, do not produce any policy or programme documents based on research into the views of their voters. Instead, all matters, including the long-term vision of parties, their ideologies, what they consider to be the key challenges facing the country and how the parties hope to tackle them – matters which would normally constitute policy positions – are addressed in party manifestoes and even in party constitutions. These documents are later distributed from the party headquarters to all party structures all the way down to grassroots level.

D. Party funding

As organisations, political parties need financial resources to manage their affairs. As one author points out, 'access to resources is a decisive factor in electoral contests and party existence … the amount of funding available determines the quality of campaigning as well as the level of communication that the party has with voters'. Public funding of political parties serves to enhance the institutional capacity of parties and enables them to compete on a more or less equal footing. However, there is a debate on the value of party funding. There are those who argue that bolstering the institutional capacity of parties could lead to undesirable consequences such as enriching political leaders, the mushrooming of political parties, the undermining of the efforts of individual parties to raise funds for themselves, and unaccountable disbursement of funds by corrupt politicians. In his study of Botswana's political parties, Tsieargues that state funding of opposition parties 'will not be a panacea for opposition', since, in the run-up to the 2009 elections in Botswana, Kgalagadi Breweries 'donated a sizeable amount of money to all political parties contesting the elections. Still, the opposition performed poorly. ' He surmises that future state funding of political parties is likely to benefit the ruling Botswana Democratic Party, as the amount of money given to parties is based on their share of the total vote in previous elections. This system could therefore have an effect of continuously marginalising smaller parties. Until the National Assembly Electoral Act, 2011, was passed by Parliament, political parties in Lesotho did not receive 'party funding' from the public purse for their daily operations. Each one of them had to source its own funds. The only financial assistance they received from the state was funding for campaigning and payment of their party agents. Under sections 70 and 71 of this act, however, political parties are entitled to both party funding and campaign funding from the public purse.

The main difference between these two types of funding, as their names suggest, is that party funding finances the day-to-day running of each party, while campaign funding is exclusively for the financing of activities related to campaigning during elections. Party funding is provided on condition that parties must have participated in elections and is based on the number of seats secured by each party. The parties must also have gained votes of not less than the threshold of 500 required for their registration with the IEC. The funding may also be provided for political parties that did not participate in the last elections, and this is also based on the threshold of 500. Even those parties which have formed alliances are still entitled to public funding, but this is allocated to each party individually. 145 A positive move with the potential of enhancing the capacity of political parties registered with the IEC under the new law is that parties now receive funding from the state based on the number of votes they received in the previous elections. 146 The danger, however, is that, if they are wholly reliant on this funding, and do not make an effort to raise funds or are unable to raise further funding, they will remain unable to compete effectively with bigger parties.

To ensure that the public money disbursed to political parties and independent candidates is accounted for by the recipients, the IEC has a right to inspect all their records. However, the campaign funding provided by the state is not sufficient to cover all campaign activities. As Makoa notes, the biggest challenge confronting Lesotho's political parties is limited financial and human-capital resources to travel around the country, recruit more members and sell their policies. Similarly, Matlosa and Sello observe that lack of public funding hinders the institutional development of political parties; hence they recommend that the Lesotho government introduce public funding based on the number of parliamentary seats occupied by political parties in Parliament. The point worth emphasising is that, although Lesotho's political parties do receive some money from the public purse, this is exclusively for campaign funding.

Other than the campaign funding that the state contributes to political parties, the National Assembly Electoral Act, 2011, also allows private funding of political parties, with the proviso that they must declare all the sources of such donations, and the value of such donations, to the IEC.

The act provides, in section 70, that:

1. For the purpose of financing its campaign, a political party registered with the Commission may raise donations from any person or organization in or outside Lesotho.

2. A source of funds or donation exceeding M200,000 [US$28 571. 43] or such amount as the Commission may, by notice published in the Gazette, determine, shall, within a period of 7 days of its receipt, be disclosed to the Commission by the Treasurer of the political party concerned.

As friendly to political parties as these sections appear to be, many of Lesotho's miniscule political parties have not been able to secure funding from external sources. This is because, according to Makoa, external donors tend to fund political parties with a chance of winning elections. He notes that Lesotho's political parties historically received aid from the then competing Eastern and Western blocs, with the BCP having benefitted from the former and the BNP having been favoured by the latter.

The strength of the political party system

Lesotho's political system has been characterised by fierce, but democratically healthy, competition between the main opposition BCP and the ruling BNP, attributable largely to the share of the parliamentary vote these two secured in the 1965 poll. Consequently, there was general optimism that the country was on course to establishing democratic rule. But the newly founded political system had to contend with an unfavourable political culture and weak state institutions, which have still not fully developed after 45 years of independence. The BNP's drastic move to annul the 1970 electoral outcome and its declaration of a state of emergency, as well as suspension of the country's Constitution and introduction of a de facto one-party system (1970–1986), among others, led to the demise of what would arguably have become a positive start for a multi-party system.

The military's forceful ousting of the BNP regime in 1986 ushered in another form of undemocratic political behaviour, which was to last from 1986 to 1993, when the military junta was eventually pressurised by internal forces composed largely of trade unions, non- governmental organisations (NGOs) and the external donor community to return the country to a pluralist system. The replacement of the military junta by the popularly elected BCP government brought a new political system, albeit of a different character from that of the immediate post- independence epoch. It was a system of one-party dominance in which the BCP became a hegemonic force after sweeping all parliamentary seats following the 1993 transitional poll. This one-party dominant system became a defining feature of Lesotho's politics even after the BCP was relegated to the opposition ranks in 1997 by its splinter party, the LCD, following incessant internal power struggles within the BCP. The LCD itself was also bedevilled by similar internal problems, leading to its splitting into the Lesotho People' Congress (LPC) in 2001 and later into the ABC in 2006. Despite these splits, however, the LCD has managed to maintain its dominance of the country's political system, with a now severely fragmented and weak opposition unable to pose any meaningful electoral threat even after the ABC's relatively good electoral performance.

Since Lesotho returned to multi-party politics in 1993, there has been a proliferation of political parties owing largely to the liberal legal framework, which allows for their easy establishment and registration. Many of these parties, however, have not been able to field candidates in all constituencies or even win votes sufficient to secure any parliamentary representation. The following tables illustrate the performance of the parties which have contested parliamentary elections since the 1993 transition to multi-party politics. In 1993, the three oldest political parties, namely the BCP, the BNP and the MFP received only about a quarter of the total vote, as reflected in Table 1.

Table 1: 1993 Lesotho general election results

Party	Votes	% Votes	Seats
BCP	398 355	74.7	65
BNP	120 686	22.6	0
MFP	7 650	1.4	0

others	6 287	1.2	0
Total	**532 978**	**99.9**	**65**

The election results in Table 1 demonstrate two things about political parties in Lesotho during this time. One is that the winning BCP was very strong relative to its opponents and was also very popular among the voters. The reason for this is widely regarded as the uncompromising will of the voters to punish the BNP for annulling the 1970 results and instituting an authoritarian, de facto, one-party system in Lesotho for 16 years. Secondly, the BNP had shrunk significantly in popularity among the voters, while the MFP had also remained politically insignificant.

The internal power struggle within the ruling BCP led to a split and to the formation of the LCD in June 1997, which also assumed power until the end of that parliamentary term. When the next elections were held in 1998, the LCD emerged victorious, as indicated by the results in Table 2.

Table 2: 1998 National Assembly election results

Party	Votes	% Votes	Seats	% Seats
LCD	355 049	60.7	78	98.73
BNP	143 073	24.5	1	1.27
BCP	61 793	10.5	0	0.00
MFP	7 460	1.4	0	0.00
others	17 365	3.0	0	0.00

| Total | 584 740 | 100.00 | 79 | 100.00 |

The 1998 results show the strength of the newly formed LCD relative not only to its progenitor, the BCP, but also to the rest of the opposition. The collective opposition had only a 39.4% share of the total vote in relation to the 60.7% of the LCD. The opposition protested the outcome of the poll and embarked on a series of actions intended to annul the results, and it also sought the support of the King to achieve its objective. The situation became highly unstable and violent until the embattled LCD leader and Lesotho's Prime Minister asked the Southern African Development Community (SADC) to intervene militarily to restore law and order.

The SADC mediation found fault not in the manner in which the poll was conducted (the joint opposition alleged fraud), but in the First-Past-The-Post (FPTP) voting system. The outcome of the mediation effort was the introduction of the Mixed Member Proportional (MMP) voting system. This new system was intended to produce a Parliament inclusive of opposition and nearly all votes in the country, as the erstwhile FPTP system had excluded the main opposition despite securing above 20% of the total vote in the 1993 and 1998 polls. Consequently, the next elections were held in 2002 under the new MMP system. The results of the 2002 elections are reflected in Table 3. The outcome of the elections was generally accepted by the opposition, as many politically significant parties obtained parliamentary representation. Under the new

electoral system, Lesotho seems to have found a long-sought formula for political stability.

Table 3: 2002 National Assembly election results

Party	Votes	% Votes	FPTP seats	PR seats	Total seats	% Seats
LCD	304316	54.8	79	0	79	65.8
BNP	124234	22.4	0	21	21	17.5
LPC	32046	5.8	1	4	5	4.2
NIP	30346	5.5	0	5	5	4.2
BAC	16095	2.9	0	3	3	2.5
BCP	14584	2.7	0	3	3	2.5
LWP	7788	1.4	0	1	1	0.8
MFP	6890	1.2	0	1	1	0.8
PFD	6330	1.1	0	1	1	0.8
NPP	3985	1.1	0	1	1	0.8
others	7772	1.4	0	0	0	1.4
Total	554386	99.9	80	40	120	99.9

However, internal power struggles, which have proved to be an enduring feature of Lesotho's political parties, and especially of the ruling parties since the 1993 elections, occurred again within the ruling LCD in October 2006, when the ABC was formed by some 17 former LCD Members of Parliament (MPs). The formation of this new party forced the Prime Minister to call a snap election in February 2007. The results of the 2007 elections are reflected in Table 4.

Table 4: 2007 National Assembly election results

Party/ Alliance	PR votes	Constituencies won	Compensatory seats	Total seats	% votes	PR% Total seats
LCD	0	62	0	62	0.0	51.67
NIP	229	0	21	21	51.8	17.50
ABC	0	17	0	17	0.0	14.17
LWP	107	0	10	10	24.3	8.33
BNP	29 965	0	3	3	6.8	2.50
ACP	20 263	1	1	2	4.6	1.67
PFD	15 477	0	1	1	3.5	0.83
BCP	9 823	0	1	1	2.2	0.83
MFP	9 129	0	1	1	2.1	0.83
BDNP	8 783	0	1	1	2.0	0.83
BBDP	8 474	0	1	1	1.9	0.83
NLFP	3 984	0	1	1	0.9	0.0
Total	442	79	40	120	100.1	99.99

The statistics in Tables 1 to 4 reflect a continuing decay rather than growth of Lesotho's political parties. While other people may use the number of paid-up members of political parties to determine their relative strength or growth, as Kadima, Matlosa and Shale have done, it is perhaps more plausible to use the actual number of votes parties obtain in elections as a measure of the real strength of parties in the case of Lesotho. This is because opposition parties do not have reliable and up-to-date membership registers. It is also important to reiterate that

Lesotho's parties have a history lacking in internal democracy and with the absence of conflict-resolution mechanisms. This results in splits and counter-splits and a disturbing proliferation of parties which are ultimately so weak that they cannot hope to win power and govern the country.

As early as the pre-independence era, the BNP and the MFP split from the BCP and contested it in the 1965 elections, with the BNP winning the election. In 1993, when democratic order was reintroduced, the BCP trounced all its opponents by sweeping all 65 seats and 74.7% of the total vote. It was followed hopelessly by its arch rival, the BNP, with only 22% votes and 0 seats, while the MFP only managed 1.2% of the vote and 0 seats. This clearly indicates how extremely weakened these two parties had become – the BNP lost 29.1% or over half its strength in 1965, and the MFP's strength declined by 5.4%.

The next poll was in 1998 following yet another split, spawned by internal conflict and power struggle, of the then ruling BCP into the LCD, and results indicate, again, that the opposition parties, including the BCP, continued to be weakened. We know the unfortunate developments that followed this election and there is no need to repeat them here, safe to say that the MMP electoral system was introduced and applied in the 2002 elections.

In the next poll in 2002, the number of parties had increased due to even more splits, especially within the 'Congress family', and they fared as follows: having won 54. 8% as opposed to the 60. 8% it obtained in 1998, the LCD declined by 5. 9% in terms of popular support and got 77 seats in the now 120-seat National Assembly. It was followed by the BNP with 22. 4% of the vote – an effective decline of 2. 1%. The rest of the votes were shared by eight remaining parties. The general trend, however, is that most of the opposition parties were too miniscule to pose any electoral threat to the LCD.

Snap elections were called in February 2007 by the Prime Minister, again following internal problems which the party was unable to resolve amicably. The elections were contested on the basis of pre-election alliances entered into by the main two parties, the LCD/National Independence Party (NIP) and the ABC/Lesotho Workers Party (LWP) respectively. The formation of these alliances was a product of leadership action without popular mandate. The membership of these parties was carefully instructed during rigorous election campaigns by the leadership to vote for their junior partners on the Proportional Representation (PR) ballot and for the main parties on the FPTP ballot.

These electoral pacts plunged the country into crisis and it took almost four years before it could be resolved through constitutional amendment. Without going into the detailed results of the poll, owing to controversies shrouding them, it suffices to indicate that the LCD/NIP and ABC/LWP earned, unfairly to other parties, a total of 82 and 27 seats under the PR and FPTP ballots respectively. Yet, if the model had been properly applied, the results would have been as follows: the LCD/NIP alliance 51. 1%; the ABC/LWP alliance 24. 4%; the BNP 6. 7%; the Alliance of Congress Parties (ACP) 4. 2%; with the remaining 12. 6% shared by small parties. This outcome does not conceal the diminishing popular support for all parties, save the ABC, which did relatively well by winning a record 17 constituencies in the post-1993 electoral history of the country. Yet the performance of the ABC notwithstanding, the current state of these parties reflects a decline rather than growth in terms of electoral performance. The situation has equally not led to an improvement or strengthening of democracy and very much reflects the pre-2007 status quo. A few indicators are in order here. The opposition is not able, under the current circumstances, to hold the ruling party accountable for the use of public resources. This is attributable to the numerical preponderance of the ruling LCD in Parliament and the use of its dominance to bulldoze bills through the House without rigorous debate.

The 2012 elections were held against the backdrop of continued internal feuds within the LCD, which culminated in yet another split of the party and in the formation of the Democratic Congress (DC). The emergence of the DC follows the same pattern as the birth of the LCD in 1997. It is led by the former leader of the LCD and former Lesotho Prime Minister, Pakalitha Mosisili, who followed the same strategy as his former leader and former Lesotho Prime Minister Ntsu Mokhehle. They both broke away from the parties in Parliament under whose banner they were elected as Prime Ministers. Both the LCD in 1997 and the DC in February 2012 were proclaimed as the government by the Speakers of the National Assembly, Teboho Kolane and Ntlhoi Motsamai, on the argument that they constituted a majority in Parliament. While the LCD had a higher majority of 41 or 63% of seats in Parliament, the DC had a relatively slim majority of 45 of the FPTP seats. The decision of the Speaker that the DC was a majority and thus a government on the basis of the FPTP seats only was hugely controversial, provoking massive protests by the opposition MPs in Parliament, but to little avail. The seats of the DC were increased a few days later to 66 by the PR MPs, who had been elected under the list of its coalition partner, the NIP.

When the elections were held on 26 May 2012, the DC contested the poll without the NIP and managed to secure a total of 48 seats (41 FPTP and 7 PR). The rest of the seats were shared by other parties, with the ABC coming in second with a total of 30 seats, the LCD emerging third with 26 seats, and the BNP in fourth position with five seats, and the other smaller parties sharing the remaining seats. For detailed results, see Table 5.

Table 5: 2012 National Assembly election results

Party	Party votes	Party's quota of votes	Allocation based of full quota	Constituency seats won the party	Party's by provisional allocation of	Total number of seats
ABC	138	30.21	30	26	4	30
BBDP	2 440	0.53	0	0	1	1
BCP	2 531	0.55	1	0	1	1
BDNP	3 433	0.75	0	0	1	1
BNP	23	5.17	5	0	5	5
DC	218	47.49	47	41	7	48
LCD	121	26.33	26	12	14	26
LPC	5 021	1.09	1	0	1	1
LWP	2 408	0.52	0	0	1	1
MFP	3 300	0.72	0	0	1	1
NIP	6 880	1.50	1	0	2	2
PFD	11 166	2.43	2	1	2	3
others	12		0	0	0	0
Total	551			80	40	120

The results in Table 5 indicate some major changes in the party and political system of the country. The ABC realised a steady growth by winning a total of 30 seats (26 from the constituencies, mostly from the central districts of Maseru and Berea, and four PR seats) and improved its performance from 17 seats in the 2007 elections. The BNP also made some small gains through the PR component of the electoral system by securing five seats, while the LCD suffered a severe blow as a result of the split of the DC, especially in its constituency-based seats.

The LCD won a total of 26 seats (12 from the constituencies, mostly from the Leribe district and home of its leader, and 14 more PR seats). It then became the biggest beneficiary of the MMP system. Although only four months old at the time of the elections (28 February to 26 May 2012), the DC did well by winning a total of 48 seats, thereby becoming by far the biggest opposition party in the post-1993 electoral politics of Lesotho. It also made history not only in Lesotho, but in Africa, by accepting the outcome of elections and handing over power to the new coalition government of the ABC, the LCD and the BNP. The new government is led by Prime Minister Tom Motsoahe Thabane, the leader of the ABC. He is deputised by Mr Mothejoa Metsing of the LCD.

Party organisation and membership

Political parties in Lesotho have constitutions which contain elaborate organisational structures, processes and procedures. These constitutions are largely similar in content owing to the fact that most of the parties are splinter parties. This further explains the similarities of their manifestos and party colours, the latter basically only being differentiated by the order and arrangement of these colours in party flags. Most of the parties have well-defined structures, processes and procedures as to how leaders are to be elected and how candidates are to be nominated. By and large, the parties provide space for their members to elect leaders at various levels through a secret-ballot system. The outcome of the electoral process for middle-ranking party committees and structures is generally respected by the parties. The difference comes, however, when people are nominated for national elections. The process involves different structures of the parties holding primary elections in line with their constitutions. The names of the victors in this process are then forwarded to the respective NECs, which are supposed to endorse these results. Instead, however, tight control and patronage is exercised during the passage of these elections through the various levels and structures of many of these parties. The primary objective of these actions is to ensure that only those who do not express a dissenting view from the leadership get elected, thereby ensuring no threat to the leaders.

Conclusion and recommendations

The constitutional and legal framework in Lesotho is conducive to political parties registering and carrying out their business. The process of registering parties is so easy that it has resulted in a 'proliferation of political parties' without adding any value to the democratic content and quality of the country. This is especially the case after Lesotho adopted a new voting system in 2001. The IEC has taken strong steps to de-register some of these parties. All these political parties are embroiled in unhelpful wrangling each time the country approaches elections. Rather than growing and evolving into strong organisations that can properly perform the functions of political parties in the democratic interest of voters, most parties witness splits and counter-splits, with these entering into opportunistic pre-election pacts. The purpose of the pacts is nothing more than an instrument for political elites to gain access to Parliament and to the material and societal benefits that accompany parliamentary positions.

Key recommendations:

- The IEC should not relent in its efforts to enforce the electoral law so that the country can produce organisations properly befitting the label of 'political parties'. This could assist in creating a competitive political atmosphere in which only serious political parties compete for citizens' votes on the basis of better policy programmes.

- Parliament should amend the electoral law to allow citizens of Lesotho outside the country to vote, as do those on foreign diplomatic missions.

Chapter Seven

The legislature

This chapter focuses on the legislative arm of government in Lesotho and describes and analyses its legal framework, membership, law-making and oversight functions, committees, public participation in its work, and the control and audit of its finances.

Legal framework

The Lesotho Parliament is established by the Constitution and electoral law, which together form its constitutional and legal framework. The Constitution provides that 'there shall be a Parliament which shall consist of the King, a Senate, and a National Assembly'. Parliament is vested with powers to make laws, but it may confer power on any authority or person to make rules, regulations, bye-laws, orders or other instruments with legislative effects. In order for any legislation to be adopted, it must be passed by both Houses of Parliament and assented to by the King to become law. The procedure for proposing and passing legislation follows steps involving three readings. First, bills are introduced to the House by Ministers, are distributed among Members of Parliament (MPs) without debate, and are then referred to the relevant portfolio committees for scrutiny and consultation with relevant stakeholders. This stage is called the First Reading of the bill. The portfolio committee concerned proposes such amendments as it deems necessary and prepares a report on the bill, which is then presented to the House for adoption. The bill then passes to the Second Reading stage, where MPs debate its general principles. The whole House constitutes itself into a Committee and debates the bill clause by clause and makes amendments as may be necessary. The Speaker makes announcements that the bill has been passed with or without amendments. The bill the passes to the Third Reading, which is the final stage in the National Assembly, after which it is passed to the Senate where a similar process is followed. After the Third Reading in the Senate, bills are returned to the National Assembly for consideration with or without further amendments. If there is disagreement between the two Houses, the decision of the National Assembly takes precedence, except on bills requiring a two- thirds majority of both Houses of Parliament. As a last stage, bills then obtain royal assent and become acts of Parliament. Executive appointments

(i. e. those of Ministers and Assistant Ministers) are effectively the prerogative of the Prime Minister, who provides mandatory advice to the King to make such appointments. 158 These appointments are not confirmed by the legislature. However, the executive is answerable as a collective to the legislature. The Constitution provides that:

The functions of the Cabinet shall be to advise the King in the government of Lesotho, and the Cabinet shall be collectively responsible to the two Houses of Parliament for any advice given to the King by or under the general authority of the Cabinet and for all things done by or under the authority of any Minister in the execution of his office. 159 The Prime Minister is constitutionally empowered to declare a 14-day state of emergency, acting in accordance with the advice of the Council of State. The period of a state of emergency can be extended, with the approval of each of the two Houses of Parliament, for a period of six months. But in cases where the two Houses do not agree, the resolution of the National Assembly prevails. 160 The National Assembly has powers to cause the removal of the Prime Minister from office by passing a vote of no confidence in his/her government, in which case the King may remove the Prime Minister from office, acting in accordance with the advice of the Council of State. If such a step is taken by the National Assembly, the Prime Minister has to either resign his/her position within three days after such a step, or advise the King to dissolve Parliament. 161 For the first time in its post-independence history, the Parliament of Lesotho took the unprecedented first steps of considering a vote of no confidence in a Prime Minister. A motion of no confidence was tabled on 6 February 2012, as outlined in case study 3.

MPs elected on the principle of the First-Past-The-Post (FPTP) system are allowed to cross the floor and to join another party in Parliament. This has indeed happened many times since the 1993 transitional elections. However, the Proportional Representation (PR) MPs are not allowed by law to change their parties. The floor-crossing practice caused a lot of controversy in 1997 when the then ruling Lesotho Congress for Democracy (LCD) abandoned the Basutoland Congress Party (BCP) under whose banner it was elected. But given the fact that the FPTP system allows elected representatives the freedom to act in a manner that promotes the interests of their constituencies, to whom they are accountable – and beyond those of any other group, including their own political parties – this may be regarded as democratic. Public opinion on this issue differed, with those supporting the move of the LCD applauding it and those opposed to the LCD condemning it. That the PR MPs are not allowed to cross the floor may be regarded as appropriate, because their accountability lies with the parties that appointed them to Parliament by having placed their names on the party's list just prior to the election.

Attempted vote of no confidence in the government of Lesotho

on Tuesday, 6 February 2012, two opposition MPs, Messrs sello Maphalla and VM Malebo tabled a motion before the Clerk of the National Assembly, in line with parliamentary procedures, the essence and content of which was to propose a vote of no confidence in the government of Lesotho. The motion read:

MOTION OF NO CONFIDENCE IN THE GOVERNMENT OF LESOTHO

That this Honourable House has no confidence in the Government of Lesotho and that this House proposes the name of Hon. Mothejoa Metsing, who is a member of the National Assembly, for His Majesty to appoint as Prime Minister in the place of the incumbent holder of the office of Prime Minister. It is to be so because instability in the ruling political party has grossly affected the stability of the Kingdom of Lesotho. Further, corruption, confusion and politicization of public servants have badly affected service delivery.

The motion was duly forwarded to the Business Committee on Tuesday, 7 February 2012, and it was considered by this Committee on Wednesday, 8 February 2012. But Hon. Mothejoa

Metsing wrote a letter to the speaker of the National Assembly on 8 February 2012 which stated:

> I have seen a copy of a motion of no confidence in the government of Lesotho which purports to nominate me as the new head of government. I submit that my name should be deleted or withdrawn from that motion as I was not consulted by the movers of the motion.

In his speech to the National Assembly, the Leader of the House, Chairperson of the Business Committee and Deputy Prime Minister, Mr Lesao Lehohla, indicated that Mr Metsing's letter meant that the motion had fallen away. should the motion have been debated and passed, the process itself and its outcome would have been unprecedented in the political history of Lesotho. Had it succeeded, and the Prime Minster advised the King to dissolve Parliament and call another election, the King could have acted as advised in terms of section 83(4) of the Constitution. Alternatively, if he (the Prime Minister) believed the motion would not be in the interest of Lesotho, he could have refused to dissolve Parliament, acting in accordance with the advice of the Council of state in terms of the Constitution, section 83(4)(a). But the Council of state is composed of people who are mostly de facto appointees of the Prime Minister, in that he/she advises the King on their appointment. Thus it would not be a simple issue for the Council of state to advise the King to act in a manner that is inconsistent with the wishes of the Prime Minister. This case shows the complexity of the process of removing a Prime Minister from office in Lesotho.

Membership

The Senate or the Upper House of Parliament is established under section 55 of the Constitution and is made up of 33 members, that is, 22 Principal Chiefs and 11 other Senators nominated by the King, acting on the advice of the Council of State. 163 Each of the Principal Chiefs has powers to designate any other person to be a Senator on his/her behalf either generally or for a specific sitting of the Senate through a written notice to the President of the Senate. 164 The Lower House or the National Assembly is composed of 80 members elected in the constituencies under the FPTP voting system. 165 However, following the electoral and constitutional reforms that were introduced in 2001, another set of 40 seats was created, thereby enlarging the House to 120 members. These seats are allocated on the basis of the PR principle to compensate for disproportionality emanating from the FPTP system.

The total number of women in the post-2007 elections Parliament was 37 (seven in the Senate and 30 in the National Assembly), thus constituting 24. 18% of the whole membership. The figure increased marginally after the 2012 elections to 40 or

26. 14% of the entire legislature (nine in the Senate and 31 in the National Assembly). This puts Lesotho below the Southern African Development Community (SADC) quota of 50% women by 2015, and there is no way it can achieve this target, because the next election will ordinarily only be held in 2017, unless a snap election is called. At the level of political parties, the National Assembly Electoral Act, 2011, attempts to ensure that representation of women, the youth and disabled persons in political activities is improved. This is done by encouraging all political parties registering with the Independent Electoral Commission (IEC), for the purpose of contesting elections, to facilitate full participation of these groups on an equal basis by: ensuring their free access to public political meetings, facilities and venues; respecting their rights to freely communicate with political parties; and generally refraining from forcing them to adopt a particular political position or to engage in, or refrain from engaging in, any political activity, other than out of their own free choice. 166While in other countries ethnicity may be an issue, which may produce undesirable political outcomes such as instability or even civil wars if not handled with care, this does not apply to Lesotho because of the general homogeneous nature of its society. As such, the issue of ethnic inclusivity of Parliament does not arise.

Membership of the National Assembly is fairly open to ordinary citizens of Lesotho, in terms of the Constitution and the electoral law. Both of these instruments provide that every person who is a registered voter and is able to speak, read and write Sesotho or English well enough to take an active part in the proceedings of both Houses of Parliament, and who is not incapacitated by physical disability, qualifies for membership of Parliament. 167 These criteria have resulted in some people who have limited formal qualifications securing membership of Parliament, invariably resulting in low-calibre MPs and a low quality of parliamentary debate. The same situation applies to the Senate. Most of the Principal Chiefs who are in the Senate have almost similar educational backgrounds to those of the MPs. 168 Consequently, some MPs in 2004 recommended that the calibre of MPs be improved through a policy that emphasises higher educational qualifications for MPs so as to increase their appreciation and comprehension of not only the challenges confronting the nation, but also their responsibility as leaders of the nation. Lesotho's MPs receive some training in the form of short-term workshops held both internally and outside the country. Internal workshops are routinely held, especially for parliamentary committees such as the Public Accounts Committee. These workshops are run by locally resourced persons with expertise in the relevant areas. The external workshops are usually organised by the Commonwealth after every election. Lesotho conducts parliamentary elections every five years, and every MP who contests elections under the FPTP system, irrespective of educational qualifications, may or may not be returned to Parliament. Those who enter Parliament through the PR component of the voting system can be (and, indeed, some of them have been) returned to Parliament by their respective parties. As such, some MPs, especially those from the ruling party, have been in Parliament since the 1993 transitional elections. However, those from the opposition parties have only been in Parliament since the introduction of the MMP system in 2002.

The members of the legislature receive by far the most extensive and lucrative remuneration packages and support, given the economic conditions of the country and relative to other public servants, such as university lecturers. The MPs are entitled to the following benefits:

- Annual salary of M266 292 (USD38 041. 71);
- A housing allowance worth M2 000 (USD285. 71) per month;
- A motor mileage allowance for vehicle use for official business;

- A tax-free allowance for electricity, telephone, cellular phone and water at the rate of M2 000 (USD285. 71) per month;

- An expense allowance to the amount of M1 000 (USD142. 86) per month;

- A sitting allowance of M150 (USD21. 43) per day;

- A constituency allowance worth M400 (USD57. 14) for the lowlands and M600 (USD85. 71) per month for the highlands;

- An interest-free loan worth M500 000 (USD71 428. 57);

- Official air travel in business class and a 100% per diem and a 10% entertainment allowance; and A tax-free gratuity at a rate of 25% of gross salary at the end of the contract.

The legislators however do not receive any research support. But Parliament itself obtains secretarial services from staff drawn from the general public service. In addition, those elected from the constituencies are also served by Constituency Secretaries. Members of the opposition parties do indeed criticise laws and policies proposed by the executive and propose their own subjects for debate. But their proposals are routinely rejected by members of the ruling party by way of using their majority. Opposition MPs are sometimes not allowed to speak by the Speaker. This happens when the ruling party wants to push through an issue in Parliament without debating it. Lesotho's Speaker of the National Assembly is elected by the National Assembly from among the members of the House or the citizens in terms of section 63 of the Constitution. He/she is not obliged to resign from party politics as is the case, for example, in the United Kingdom. This makes the Speaker susceptible to party-political influence. Members of the ruling party are also forced to adhere strictly to the party line by the Chief Whip, and they do not criticise the executive. There are likely to be changes in the manner in which the Speaker runs Parliament and manages debates in Parliament after the 2012 elections, since Lesotho now has a new Speaker. The Speaker has been elected by 71 MPs from the three parties which have formed the coalition government and a group of other MPs (calling themselves 'the Bloc') drawn from parties which are not part of the coalition government.

Law-making and oversight

Although legislative houses in democracies ought to be a location for serious debate and decision- making about issues of national importance, the Lesotho Parliament has been hamstrung by the dominance of the ruling party since 1993. In the period between the 1993 and 2002 elections, the ruling party enjoyed almost exclusive membership of the National Assembly, with often only one member, or very few members, of the opposition present in the House. Under such conditions, there was arguably little serious debate on national issues.

The introduction of the Mixed Member Proportional (MMP) system led to a more inclusive Parliament, in that a significant number of opposition members joined Parliament, but even then this did not lead to Parliament becoming a house of debate. Instead, according to some opposition MPs interviewed in 2004, 'Parliament is not a genuine debating forum; '...the ruling LCD uses its majority to forestall democratic debates on important national issues, and ...bills are passed into law before they have been properly scrutinised or seriously debated'. The Parliament of Lesotho has not realised any significant improvement in the quality of debate since the 2007 elections. Although one veteran MP agreed that 'Parliament is supposed to be a debating chamber', another opposition MP affirmed the assertion that Lesotho's legislature does not debate issues. He indicated that the ruling party's MPs always tend to call what is notoriously dubbed a '4. 2' when issues have to be thoroughly debated. This is a Parliamentary Standing Order usually invoked to indicate that an issue has been sufficiently debated, even when no debate has taken place, and it is time to vote. In the end, the Lesotho

Parliament is merely a 'rubber-stamp' of the decisions of the executive. This situation is likely to change given the composition of the post-2012 elections Parliament, which has a numerically strong opposition (the DC [Democratic Congress]). The DC MPs arguably also have better experience and technical knowledge given that many of them were Ministers and heads of government ministries or occupied other senior levels in the public service.

The Lesotho legislature is in session from the first week of February to the last week of May and breaks for two weeks during the Easter holidays. It resumes in the first week of September up to the last week of November, after which it takes a two-week break to commemorate Lesotho's independence. This adds up to about 196 work days a year. Its 2007–2012 session considered a total of 92 bills and 205 motions. Many of these bills have since been passed into acts of Parliament. Of these bills, at least three are considered to have been of considerable national importance, given their cultural, economic and political impact on the nation, and generated intense debates. These were the Land Bill, 2009, the Public Meetings and Processions Bill, 2009, and the National University of Lesotho (Amendment) Bill, 2011. Despite these debates, the ruling party simply used its majority to push the latter two bills through the National Assembly, and this even after the opposition had walked out as a sign of protest. The essence of the Land Bill, 2009, was that it changed the land-tenure system from customary tenure to private ownership, which would allow foreign enterprises to own land in Lesotho. It also provided for land appropriation by the state for reasons of failing to use land productively. The bill was criticised by different sectors of the population for the limited public consultation that had taken place and for the removal of traditional chiefs from the land-allocation process – a serious reversal of long-standing tradition and custom in the country.

The second bill of importance passed was the Public Meetings and Processions Bill, 2009, which is now an act of Parliament (Public Meetings and Processions Act, 2010). This act effectively makes the holding of public meetings and processions illegal if they are held without the permission of the police and chiefs. It makes it mandatory for anyone wishing to hold public meetings or processions in urban areas to apply for a permit to do so, to the officer commanding the police in the case of urban areas or to the headman or his representative in the case of rural areas. The application must be made at least seven days before such an event or at least two days in the case of urgent meetings or processions. These officers are empowered to either grant or refuse permission, depending on their assessment of the security situation and the general threat to public security and public order. They are also empowered to cancel such permits or impose conditions in relation to such events if the they believe that the event poses a threat or harm to public peace, public safety, public security or public order. This is a significant departure from an earlier arrangement in which citizens were required to only notify the police of where and when they wanted to hold meetings, political rallies, public processions and demonstrations. The public's right to freedom of assembly and association has been considerably diminished by subjecting them to state approval and prior restraint as a result of this law.

The last bill, for this purpose, is the National University of Lesotho (Amendment) Bill, 2011, which was passed by the Senate after going through the National Assembly in December 2011. This bill seeks to amend section 49 of the National University of Lesotho Order, 1992, so that management of the University can fire its employees in terms of the provisions of the national Labour Code Order, 1992. Prior to the bill, employees of the University were governed by the National University of Lesotho Order, 1992. During the parliamentary debate on the bill, the opposition MPs walked out of Parliament on the grounds that more public consultations were needed on the bill, since it would give the university management excessive powers to dismiss staff of the university at will. Opposition MPs were united in opposing the bill and a division was summarily called so that the National Assembly would formally vote on the bill, effectively stopping further debate. At this stage, the opposition walked out as a sign that they did not agree with the bill. Although individual MPs are allowed to introduce private members' bills in terms of the Parliamentary Standing Orders, all bills have thus far been introduced by the executive. This is because, according to Thabisi, opposition MPs lack the requisite expertise and legal capacity, while the government uses civil servants in the Law Office to draft all bills. Only one bill has so far been blocked by the Senate, since passage of a bill requires a two-thirds majority in both Houses of Parliament.

The Senators, in the case concerned, voted unanimously against the Sixth Constitutional Amendment Bill, 2008, whose object was to subject the rulings of the High Court of Lesotho on election-related disputes to appeal. The Constitution provides that the decision of the High Court in these matters is final. The ruling party wanted the Constitution to be amended so that the case, on the allocation of 40 PR seats, which was still before the High Court, could be heard by the Court of Appeal. This was a very sensitive case, which had the potential of causing the ruling party to lose a total of 21 seats, leading to a majority of only 62 in the National Assembly. The argument of the Senators was that the bill should wait until the High Court had made its ruling on the case so that the bill not be construed as an attempt to pre-empt the outcome of the case. They further argued that to pass the bill at that time would be tantamount to abuse of power by the ruling party designed to manipulate the Constitution in order to protect

its government. The ruling party had secured the two-thirds majority required to pass the bill in the National Assembly, and it had to obtain the same majority in the Senate as required by the Constitution in relation to all entrenched clauses of the Constitution. The legislature does provide effective scrutiny of the executive in two ways. One is through normal parliamentary question time, during which MPs pose written questions to Ministers for oral answers. Ministers respond to such questions on a weekly basis or, in cases of urgent questions, within two days. Another oversight mechanism is where Parliament summons Ministers and senior government officials to appear before it to answer questions concerning their respective ministries and departments. There are many cases in which the Public Accounts Committee has summoned the chief accounting officers of different ministries to explain perceived improprieties concerning the use of public resources under their authority. The Ministers are given 30 minutes in which to answer questions from the members. They face challenging questions by the MPs on government policies, although the process does not result in any positive change.

Committees

The Parliament of Lesotho features three types of committees, namely Ad Hoc Committees (established to deal with particular matters and dissolved immediately after completing their tasks), Sessional Select Committees, which are appointed for a Session of Parliament, and Portfolio Committees – established to last for the life of Parliament which oversee different ministries of government. The Sessional Select Committees include:

- The Business Committee, chaired by the Leader of the House, who is a senior Minister and currently the Deputy Prime Minister, whose function it is to determine the size of every other committee and to determine the length of time allocated for any bill and government motions;

- The Committee on Standing Orders, presided over by the Speaker to deal with rules and standing orders;

- The Public Accounts Committee (PAC), which is the watchdog over public money spent by the executive and is chaired by a member of the opposition;

- The Ethics, Code of Conduct, Immunities and Privileges Committee, whose function is to consider and investigate all complaints of alleged breaches of privilege by the House, its members, officers and the Speaker; The

HIV/AIDS Committee; and The Chair of Chairs Committee, which coordinates the work of all other committees.

In addition to these committees, the Lesotho Parliament has introduced six Portfolio Committees to oversee the activities of different ministries of the government. These are:

- The Portfolio Committee of the Social Cluster, which is responsible for the Ministries of Health and Social Welfare; Education and Training; and Gender, Youth, Sports and Recreation;

- The Portfolio Committee of the Economic and Development Cluster responsible for the Ministries of Finance and Development Planning; Trade and Industry, Cooperatives and Marketing; Employment and Labour; and Agriculture and Food Security;

- The Portfolio Committee of the Law and Public Safety Cluster responsible for the Ministries of Home Affairs and Public Safety; Justice, Human Rights and Rehabilitation; and Law and Constitutional Affairs;

- The Portfolio Committee of the Natural Resources, Tourism and Land Cluster responsible for the Ministries of Natural Resources; Tourism, Environment and Culture;

Forestry and Land Reclamation; and Public Works and Transport; and

- The Portfolio Committee on the Ministries overseen by the Prime Minister, including the Ministries of Local Government; Foreign Affairs; Communication, Science and Technology; Public Service; Defence and National Security; and Parliamentary Affairs.

The chairs of all these committees are selected by the Business Committee, which determines the size and work of other committees. Most committees are chaired by the members of the ruling LCD, except for the Public Accounts Committee, which is chaired by the leader of the opposition. These committees have powers to summon ministers and senior government officials to appear before them and answer questions relating to the functioning of their respective ministries and departments. In cases where Ministers fail to oblige, the committees can report to the House, which, in turn, can institute disciplinary action. The committees face serious resource challenges in terms of research capacity and are forced to rely on the resources of Parliament as a whole. This implies that they can hardly seek out specialised expertise to enable them to propose amendments to laws and scrutinise government policy. Such services are usually provided by professional consultants for hefty fees, which the committees cannot afford. The executive usually supplies the committees with the information they want. The committees operate on a consensus basis, though members sometimes vote in order to reach decisions. Even after voting, however, there are channels through which the views of the minority can be heard when the business under consideration is tabled in Parliament. The committees indeed criticise the government, as that is one of the main reasons for their establishment. The executive does not always implement the recommendations of the committees. However, whenever a report on a particular issue is presented to it, it is obliged to respond.

The response is normally sought by the Speaker, who writes to the Ministers concerned instructing them to respond within a stipulated time, usually 14 days. If Ministers do not respond, the Prime Minister may be approached to ensure compliance. The crucial issue, however, is that the recommendations of the committees are not binding on the executive. There are cases, nevertheless, where recommendations of committees have resulted in the significant amendment of draft laws. One recent example is the Children's Protection and Welfare Bill, 2010 (passed into law in 2011). This law originates from recommendations made by one of the committees. The Public Accounts Committee, which is responsible for examining the government's finances and budget processes, has always existed, even prior to the coming into being of other portfolio committees. However, it does not have the skills necessary to provide effective oversight of the executive, because its members do not have any kind of training for the job. The budget is presented by the Minister concerned to the Social Cluster Committee well in advance of its adoption date, and this Committee can summon the Minister or his/her officials for consultations.

Participation in the work of the legislature

Members of Lesotho's legislature enjoy opportunities to develop close links with their constituencies. These are cultivated through the traditional rallies in their respective constituencies. Indeed, some of the MPs claimed that they conduct rallies to inform the electorate about parliamentary processes, including the bills and laws passed by Parliament. However, these claims were dismissed by members of civil society organisations, who asserted that MPs do not report to the electorate during parliamentary sessions and meet with their constituencies only when they need to ask the people to return them to Parliament. The extent to which members of the legislature maintain close links with constituencies is a matter of personal choice, without any legal specifications. Some MPs maintain close links and often go back to their constituencies to hear people's views on important bills before Parliament. During these meetings, MPs become accessible to every person in the constituency and are viewed in a positive manner. As to how ordinary people view the legislature depends on the conduct of individual MPs within their constituencies. Where MPs do not maintain close links with constituencies, it stands to reason that they are not well liked. To facilitate the process of constant consultation, MPs elected under the FPTP ballot are each given a monthly Constituency Allowance and a Secretary. This Secretary is recruited by the relevant MP, but is paid by Parliament. Parliament is yet to provide resources to establish a full secretariat. 202 Parliament has further made it possible for different sectors of society to participate in law-making processes by inviting the public to make representations to relevant committees of Parliament. The latest examples of these consultations, although criticised as inadequate by civil society organisations (in terms of scope and time allowed for them), were the Land Bill, 2009, and the National University of Lesotho (Amendment) Bill, 2011.

In other countries, information about the operations of the legislature is accessed through several means, including official websites and newsletters. The use of such communication tools does not exist in Lesotho. 203 Parliament, however, has a library where ordinary members of the public can access hard copies of some documents, including the daily Hansards and Order Papers, which can be obtained on request from Parliament. The minutes of committee meetings and reports on these hearings remain privileged information that cannot even be discussed with the media until they are presented in Parliament. 204 The state-owned Radio Lesotho reports on daily parliamentary debates. Television Lesotho, too, covers parliamentary proceedings on when important issues such as the budget are tabled and discussed. The private media, on the other hand, less occasionally report on parliamentary issues when these have the potential to attract public attention. Overall, it can be said that the media does report on important issues discussed in Parliament, although not consistently enough. Examples here include the most recent budget, which received wide coverage and debate in the prominent newspapers and on radio stations. 205 Civil society can participate in the work of the legislature by presenting views to it. This can be done through raising its views with the MPs of its respective constituencies or, if invited to do so, by the portfolio committees or by way of petitioning parliament. Civil society organisations (CSOs) do normally succeed in accessing the legislature in these ways. 206 Their influence on the legislative process is, however, limited given that their submissions have virtually no impact. The ruling party passes bills without any regard to the opinions of CSOs.

Control and audit of parliamentary finances

The funds allocated to the legislature are not treated differently from those of other departments of government in terms of controls. Parliament is not financially independent from the executive; but is treated administratively as simply just another department of government. To ensure that funds allocated to the legislature are appropriately spent, the government relies on the Auditor General to compile a report for every financial year. It is not easy to discern the budgetary allocation for the legislature from the national budget, since this is not reflected clearly in the budget.

There have been allegations by the media that funds have been squandered,208 and, in some cases, the allegations have been true. There was a case of fraud in which the former Clerk of the National Assembly, Mr Matlamukele Matete, was accused and convicted of defrauding the state of M1 475 259. 29 (USD210 551. 33). He was found guilty of having inflated the price of a photocopying machine valued at only M50 000 (USD7 142. 86), which he bought for the National Assembly in 2005. He is now serving a four-year prison sentence without the option of a fine after the Court of Appeal imposed a heavier punishment than the High Court, which had sentenced him to pay a fine of M10 000 (USD1 428. 57) or up to five years in prison. Lesotho's

Parliament has no research wing, and, as such, no funds are allocated for research.

Efforts towards strengthening Parliament

The Lesotho Parliament has adopted the recommendations of a report by a consultant after conducting a study intended to improve the functioning of Parliament. significant among these recommendations was that there was a need to establish Portfolio Committees with a view to achieving the following goals, among others: the review of proposed legislation and pending bills; examination of policy issues; special investigations; encouraging consensus-building and ensuring that all views are considered on issues under discussion; holding public hearings and encouraging citizens' participation; educating citizens on important policies; holding open meetings; creating spaces for experts to present their views on important issues; and establishing access points for citizens to participate in the legislative process.

Parliament accepted these recommendations and established five Portfolio Committees, which previously did not exist. These committees have powers to hear oral evidence and call for papers, to consult and liaise with state departments, and to ensure attendance of any person at a meeting in terms of the Parliamentary Powers and Privileges Act. These committees have already begun working by calling in different stakeholders on important national issues. A recent example of this is the social Cluster Portfolio Committee, which invited key stakeholders when the National university of Lesotho (Amendment) Bill, 2011, was tabled before the National Assembly. The stakeholders included the members of the teaching and research staff who would be directly affected by the new law, as well as students, parents and university management. These committees may not yet be working as well as could be expected, but at least their establishment is a step in the right direction.

Conclusion and recommendations

The Parliament of Lesotho is weak relative to the executive, and is not able to effectively perform its key oversight functions. There is potential for change if the newly established portfolio committees can effectively perform their duties. Parliament has not been helped by the dominance of the ruling party, which denies healthy democratic debate before bills are passed, as well as enforcement of strict party discipline against MPs, who may not question or dissent from the party line. With little formal education and origins in humble communities, MPs face serious challenges in carrying out their parliamentary work. Civil society participates in the legislative process by expressing views, but is ignored by the ruling party. The following measures may help to improve and broaden political participation in Parliament:

- Parliament should ensure that the chairpersonship of portfolio committees reflects the composition of the House to avoid domination by the ruling party and government.

- The constitutional provisions regarding eligibility for election to Parliament should be carefully studied to try to ensure that candidates with relatively higher levels of education enter into office, while at the same time exercising caution against creating an elitist Parliament which is out of touch with ordinary citizens.

- Parliament should allocate more resources to itself and its portfolio committees to provide sufficient capacity for research.

- Parliament should establish close links with civil society and continue with the good practice of consultation with communities, interest and expert groups, before bills are passed.

- Parliament should establish its own Parliamentary Service Commission to deal with its own staff recruitment rather than rely on the executive for expertise.

- The staff concerned should be given capacity through appropriate training to offer support and technical guidance to portfolio committees.

Chapter Eight

Local government

Lesotho does not have regional (provincial) government structures. It has a local government system that is provided for in the Constitution, in section 106(1), and which reads: 'Parliament shall establish such local authorities as it deems necessary to enable urban and rural communities to determine their affairs and to develop themselves. Such authorities shall perform such functions as may be conferred by an Act of Parliament.'

The Constitution does not define the powers of local authorities and leaves all matters pertaining to them, including their composition, powers and responsibilities, to the applicable constitutive act of Parliament. Section 4 of the Local Government Act, 1997, establishes the local authorities and provides for the composition of the councils at four levels (community, rural, urban and municipal). However, the act also provides for the election of two traditional chiefs to serve on each council. The principle of election of the chiefs for two reserved seats on each council became controversial after the passage of this law, as it would require chiefs to stand for elections under the banner of one or other of the political parties, thereby undermining their presumed apolitical character. The government consequently changed this requirement and settled for nomination of the chiefs by their peers. This was done through the Local Government [Amendment] Act, 2004, section 4(1)(a), which provides that the chiefs are 'nominated' by other chiefs onto the councils. The Minister of Local Government and Chieftainship Affairs has powers to declare the four types of councils, namely community, rural, urban and municipal councils. In practice, the councils throughout the country are severely lacking in autonomy from the central government and are also characterised by extremely low levels of capacity. Although they are empowered by section 47 of the Local Government Act, 1997, to establish their own Council

Funds, in which all monies generated by various means (including any fines and penalties, rates, taxes, duties, fees and other charges levied, revenue from property, all donations, gifts, grants, and all funds appropriated to them by the central government) are held, no Council Funds were established throughout the period 2005 to 2011. There is no clear policy on how such funds are to be managed and accounted for by councils, as, by its own admission, the government says that councils are collecting revenue but it is not clear how the funds are to be accounted for and reported on in terms of their use. 211The result has been an extreme lack of capacity to provide services for the people. Even in a few cases where the councils have been able to collect small amounts of money in the form of charges to farmers for grazing their animals on reserved pastures, these were taken over by the central government. The councils also do not have bank accounts, despite the fact that section 48 of the Local Government Act, 1997, provides for such accounts. In the end, the councils rely heavily and without choice on the money appropriated to them by the central government, which itself is insufficient and disbursed to them too late to carry out their functions.

All local authorities are empowered to establish a Council Fund into which all finances of the respective councils are to be paid. The sources of funding are expected to come from different sources, as indicated above. However, it is clear from the data that central government has not as yet decentralised the key functions and accompanying resources to councils throughout the country. The councils depend on the central government for fiscal revenue to a very large extent, and it comes with 'strings attached', thereby denying councils the power to decide on their own expenditure. The councils are also not able to raise sufficient revenue locally. Even when they do make some collections, these are taken over by the central government. The effect of this has been extremely limited autonomy and capacity on the part of the councils, which cause much frustration for the councils and the citizens they are supposed to serve under the new dispensation.

Structure

The local government system consists of 65 community councils, 11 urban councils, one municipal council, and ten district councils in that order, making their total number 87. The membership of each community council is composed of 15 popularly elected members and two gazetted chiefs. The urban councils consist of 13 popularly elected members and not more than two gazetted chiefs. The municipal council is made up of between eight and 15 elected members and not more than three gazetted chiefs. In all cases, the chiefs must be nominated by other chiefs in each of the councils. The composition of the district councils is determined by the Minister of Local Government and Chieftainship Affairs through a notice in a Government Gazette. Similarly, the two chiefs become members of the district councils through nomination by other chiefs from within the community councils. The implication here is that local authorities in Lesotho lack autonomy from the central government. The Minister has a large amount of power over these authorities.

The district councils are headed by politically appointed District Administrators, who are followed in rank by District Council Secretaries (also appointees of the central government), while the municipal council is headed by an elected Mayor. All these councils have a life span of five years in terms of section 8 of the Local Government [Amendment Act], 2004.

The councils are empowered under the Local Government Act, 1997, section 42, to make their own bye-laws relating to an array of issues relevant to their own areas. Community councils are empowered by the Local Government [Amendment] Act, 2004, to perform the following functions:

- Control of natural resources (e. g. sand, stone) and environmental protection (e. g. dongas, pollution);
- Land/site allocation;
- Provision of minor roads (also bridle-paths); Grazing control;
- Water supply in villages (maintenance); Markets (provision and regulation); and
- Provision of burial grounds.

Other local authorities, which are not specified in the law, perform other functions beyond those listed above. These include promotion of economic development, streets and public places, parks and gardens, control of building permits, fire brigades, education, recreation and culture, roads and traffic, fencing, local administration of central regulation and licences, fencing, care of mothers, young children, the aged and integration of people with disabilities, laundries, omnibus terminals, mortuaries and burial of bodies of destitute persons and unclaimed bodies, upholding public decency and prosecuting offences against public order, agriculture services (including the improvement of agriculture), forestry (including preservation of forests), improving forests, and control of designated forests in local authority areas.

Elections

Following the 1960 district councils, which were abolished by the then Basotho National Party (BNP) government in 1968, Lesotho did not have an elected local government system until 30 April 2005 when local government elections were held under the First-Past-The-Post (FPTP) voting system. These elections ushered in a local government system based on the principle of devolution of power from the central government. The term of office of all elected councillors and the nominated chiefs was five years,217 but it was extended by 12 months to allow the

Ministry of Local Government and Chieftainship Affairs to prepare for the next elections and to resolve a number of outstanding issues before the poll. The second local government elections were held on 1 October 2011. In terms of the Local Government [Declaration of Councils] Notice, 2011, the new councils now number 86 in total.

Local government elections have not generated much interest among the voters compared with the national poll. This is demonstrated by the lower voter turnout in the last two elections of 2005 and 2011. While the national voter turnout stood at 62. 32% in 1965, 81. 9% in the 1970 annulled poll, 72. 28% in 1993, 71. 83% in 1998, 66. 69% in 2002 and 49% in 2007 respectively, the situation was different for local elections where only 30. 28%220 of the voters cast their ballots in 2005 followed by 32% in the 2011 polls. The low voter turnout in the 2005 local government elections prompted the Commonwealth Expert Team to express the following sentiments:

It was of concern to the Team that voter turnout was low. While taking cognizance of the fact that these were the first Local Government Elections, and that voters may not yet have familiarized themselves with this new electoral process, factors such as the large distances to polling stations in far flung constituencies (especially those in the Highlands) cannot be discounted. The fact that the polling day was not declared a public holiday might have contributed to a low turnout. Among the reasons cited for the apathy of voters were an overall lack of trust in political parties, and the perception among voters that their votes would not bring about any changes in the government. It was also noted that the voter turnout tended to be larger in more rural constituencies, as opposed to urban areas such as Maseru. These reasons are plausible and should be considered by the politicians so that voter turnout can be improved in the next poll in 2016. However, not much can be done, especially in the short run, about people's lack of trust in their politicians. This will take a long time to address, and politicians themselves will have to undertake serious introspection about how to win back trust. Local-government elections were a novelty in Lesotho in 2005, but, by 2011, the novelty had worn off. Issues around accessibility of polling stations may be addressed by establishing as many stations as possible. However, the main challenge here would be (or perhaps was) resource constraints. There is no indication that any of these concerns are being addressed.

The day of the election in 2011 could have been declared a public holiday if the government had accorded significance to these elections. Alternatively, these elections could also have been postponed to the same time as the national elections in 2012, since they had already been delayed by over a year. The abysmal performance of the previous councils as regards service provision may have also engendered a feeling of despondency and disillusionment on the part of voters. 223 There has been virtually no service provision in the last six years of these councils due to the fact that: (i) the central government has not decentralised the functions it earmarked for the councils under the Local Government Act, 1997; (ii) the councils lack autonomy to control their own affairs and programmes; and (iii) they lack virtually all capacity to implement their own programmes. In the end, all these factors may have contributed cumulatively to the low voter turnout in the October 2011 local elections. Some suggest that the poll coincided with other events such as the Morija Arts and Cultural Festival, which young voters may have regarded as more important than the elections. Other observers express doubts about the preparedness of the Independent Electoral Commission (IEC) for this election. They argue that the IEC had not been able to prepare a clean voters' roll and that, in some cases, two voters' rolls (old and new) were used to address the gaps in the final roll. The final voters' roll had left out a considerable number of voters. There were also instances where voters were not transferred from their original places of registration to their new places of residence. The quality and adequacy of Lesotho's voters' roll has been a matter of concern, especially for opposition parties – also in relation to parliamentary elections since 1993. A great deal of effort must be made to address this issue to ensure the credibility of both local-government and parliamentary elections in the future.

Access to information

Regulation (14) (2) of the Local Government Regulations, 2005, provides that citizens can, if they so wish, require copies of the minutes of the meetings of councils at a fee councils may prescribe. Other than this Regulation, there are no other legal provisions that provide access to information held by local authorities. Access is not generally denied to those needing some information from councils in relation to activities and records. There are as yet no official publications issued by local authorities in Lesotho. Similarly, there are no draft or final laws, policy documents and budgetary or other financial information available. However, community councils within the Maseru administrative district formulated draft bye-laws as provided for under section 42 of the Local Government Act, 1997, as amended. These, however, have not been passed by the Ministry of Local Government Chieftainship Affairs and their fate is unknown. Local authorities have never invited submissions on any official policies or documents, as these do not exist.

Oversight of local executives

The executive arm of the local government system at the Community Council level is composed of the Council Secretary as provided for under section 2 of the Local Government Act, 1997. This officer is assisted by an accounts clerk, a clerical assistant, and a messenger. The Council Secretary reports to the District Council Secretary, who, in turn, reports to the Director-General based at the national level. But, more generally, oversight over local authorities is exercised in two forms. One is that the Local Government Act, 1997, section 63, provides for auditing of all accounts of the councils by the government auditor or another qualified auditor appointed by the Minister of Local Government and Chieftainship Affairs. A commission of inquiry may also be appointed in terms of the Commissions of Inquiry Act, 1994, to make inquiries about any matter concerning the administration of any council. It seems that there are no citizen-based, democratic oversight mechanisms in respect of local executives, since the executive at this level is answerable only to the executive at national level and not to the elected local council. The national legislature does not directly perform an oversight function over the local government system. It could do so, however, through the ministry responsible by asking questions of the Minister concerned with the operations of the councils.

Participatory democracy

In theory, the introduction of the local government system was intended to promote participatory democracy at local level. The Basutoland Congress Party (BCP) had promised the Basotho nation that, if elected in 1993, it would ensure greater devolution of political power to the grassroots level through the reintroduction of democratic local government. It said in its 1993 election manifesto, for example:

The BCP is convinced that true development and good governance require grassroots involvement in both planning and decision-making. To that extent, the BCP government shall: (a) ensure the establishment of councils at district; constituency and village levels: (b) facilitate a democratic relationship between the central and local governments. Thus, as a clear commitment to a decentralised system of administration, the BCP government developed the White Paper on the Establishment of Democratic Local Government, 1996. The White Paper outlines the commitment to, and rationale and policy justification for, local government:

The present government has an unequivocal manifesto commitment to the country to introduce local government during its term of office. This political commitment is highlighted in the three objectives.

(1) Deepening and widening access to the structures of Government in Lesotho, and giving the electorate greater democratic control over development processes and making public institutions more accountable to elected representatives.

Moving decision making, resource allocation and district level planning and local development and public services physically closer to the people.

Distributing GOL's [Government of Lesotho's] human, institutional and infrastructural resources and capacity equitably across the country. Regulation (10)(4) of the Local Government Regulations, 2005, creates some space for citizens to participate in the decision-making process, though not directly. This is through opening the meetings of councils to the public, except when chairpersons or councils consider certain issues to be of a confidential nature.

In practice, citizens have not used this important opportunity, probably because they do not know it exists. There have been no public hearings where policies have been presented or civil society organisations have made inputs. There are no formal mechanisms for ensuring public consultation at community level on matters affecting different communities, nor have there been any initiatives to develop participatory budgeting. Individual councillors can, however, consult with the people in their respective electoral divisions (a cluster of villages from which a councillor is elected for a seat in a community council) through the traditional lipitso to discuss issues of importance to communities.

Conclusion and recommendations

The local government system in Lesotho is only seven years old. As such, it is still confronted with many challenges, which include serious lack of capacity to carry out its legally prescribed functions, and lack of autonomy from central government. In addition, the government has not yet decentralised many of the services to the local councils, which, by law, it should have done. It is not clear how the government will address these challenges, if at all, because no attempts in this direction have been made. In this regard, the government should grant appropriate autonomy and resources to local councils to carry out their legal mandate. It should also decentralise all services earmarked for the councils.

Chapter Nine

Traditional authorities and the institution of chieftainship

This chapter reflects on the main issues relating to the constitutional and legal recognition of the chieftainship, its role in public life, its systems of accountability, and debate on its role in Lesotho's political system.

The Basotho nation was founded on the institution of chieftainship. However, it is not clear whether the system of chieftainship emerged with the coming into power of Moshoeshoe I, the founder of the Basotho nation. Several historians indicate that there were many autonomous Basotho chiefdoms before Moshoeshoe was born, himself a member of the Bakoena ba Mokoteli chiefdom. Based on this research, which is informed largely by the works of the members of the Paris Evangelical Missionary Society (PEMS) and other historians and anthropologists, Machobane traces the evolution of the Basotho nation and highlights the central role played by the chiefs in its genesis. According to Machobane, a chief meant one who 'watched over the welfare' of those under him, governing with the assistance of a few other people in accordance with the established and practical traditional institutions and principles, and settling disputes among the people. It is clear, therefore, that, without leadership qualities, chiefs would not be chiefs. The chieftainship has survived despite several attempts by both colonial and post-colonial states to whittle away its powers, and it continues to play an extremely important part in the lives of the Basotho.

Structurally, the chiefs are arranged into four categories countrywide: Principal Chiefs (22 in number); Independent Chiefs (2); Area Chiefs (282); Chiefs (235); and Headmen (695 countrywide) All these chiefs are recognised by the state by having their names published in the Government Gazette. As a result, they receive a monthly income in the form of salaries and allowances. This is a colonial legacy left by British rule in the country.

There are also Customary Chiefs for every village, whose number is difficult to establish, since they are not legally recognised by the state through the Government Gazette.

Constitutional and legal recognition of traditional leadership

The Constitution and other laws recognise the institution of chieftainship. The Constitution, in section 103, provides that:

(a) The twenty-two offices of Principal Chief set out in Schedule 2 to this Constitution and the other offices of Chief recognised under the law in force immediately before the commencement of this Constitution shall continue to exist.

Schedule 2 referred to above stipulates the number of Principal Chiefs and their areas of jurisdiction. The Constitution provides, in section 103(2), that 'Parliament may make provision for the regulation of offices of chief', thereby subjecting the chieftainship to the authority of elected parliament. Section 103(3) further provides that 'each Chief shall have such functions as are conferred on him by this Constitution or by or under any other law'.

Official recognition of the legal status and functions of chiefs is further recognised and codified in three laws, namely the Laws of Lerotholi, the Chieftainship Act, 1968 and Order No. 26 of 1970.

The appointment of chiefs is governed by the Laws of Lerotholi. Law 1 on succession to chieftainship provides that:

Succession to the chieftainship in Basutoland shall be by right of birth, that is, the first-born male of the first wife. If the first wife has no male issue then the first-born male of the next wife in succession shall be heir to the chieftainship. Provided that if a chief dies leaving no male issue the chieftainship shall devolve upon the male following according to succession of wives. (Law 1 Succession to Chieftainship, cited in Ashton, 1952: 193)

The positions of Principal and Ward Chiefs are recognised in section 2 of Order No. 26, 1970, as well as the Laws of Lerotholi and the Chieftainship Act, 1968. The Chieftainship Act is elaborate on the procedure of chieftainship succession. Section 103(1) recognises the offices of 22 Principal Chiefs, while section 2 gives Parliament powers to make provisions for the regulation of offices of chiefs. With regard to the junior chiefs and headmen, the Chieftainship Act, 1968, Part II, recognises the offices of chiefs and their functions and spells out the hierarchical structure of the chieftainship. At the apex of this structure is a Principal Chief or Ward Chief, followed by junior chiefs. The Chieftainship Act provides that:

Each office of Chief immediately subordinate to an office of Principal or Ward Chief has authority over the other offices of Chief in its area, and that authority is exercised through the other offices of Chief that are immediately subordinate to that office, and so in descending order of the status of each office of the offices that have immediate authority without the interpretation of any other office of Chief. The Act further provides that:

It is the duty of every Chief to support, aid and maintain the King in His Government of Lesotho according to the Constitution and the other laws of Lesotho and, subject to their authority and direction, to serve the people in the area of his authority, to promote their welfare and lawful interests, to maintain public safety and public order among them, and to exercise all lawful powers and perform all lawful duties of his office impartially, efficiently and quickly according to law.

The Act further provides that:

It is the duty of every Chief to support, aid and maintain the King in His Government of Lesotho according to the Constitution and the other laws of Lesotho and, subject to their authority and direction, to serve the people in the area of his authority, to promote their welfare and lawful interests, to maintain public safety and public order among them, and to exercise all lawful powers and perform all lawful duties of his office impartially, efficiently and quickly according to law.

In addition to these general functions, each chief, beginning with the Principal and Ward Chief, has powers to issue orders to others below him, and the latter are obliged to obey those orders. It is the duty of every chief to prevent crime and he is empowered to arrest and present before the nearest court or police force any person who commits a crime. The chieftainship is further subjected to the authority of the government through the Minister responsible for Chieftainship Affairs, who has powers to give directives to the chiefs. The chiefs are obliged to obey such directives. On the question of succession to the office of chief, part III stipulates how the process must proceed, and states that a legitimate son of a chief is the lawful heir. It reads thus:

When an office of Chief becomes vacant, the firstborn or only son of the first or only marriage of the Chief succeeds to the office, and so, in descending order, that person succeeds to the office who is the firstborn or only son of the first or only marriage of a person who, but for his death or incapacity, would have succeeded to that office in accordance with the provisions of this succession. In cases where there is no successor in the first house of the chief who had more than one wife, the first-born son in the second house succeeds to that office, in that descending order as above. In circumstances where there are no surviving sons, the wives of the deceased chief in order of their seniority succeed him, or when there are no surviving wives, the legitimate eldest brother, or the eldest surviving uncle, according to customary law. What is clear from these provisions is that the senior-most legitimate sons, and not daughters, become successors to the office of chief. This is because the expectation is that daughters will get married and be cut off from their lineage as they become subsumed in the affairs of their new families. In that event, they will take their chieftainship rights to their new families, while, customarily, the institution belongs to particular families. It is also clear that the wives of chiefs have an opportunity to succeed their husbands in cases where there are no male claimants to the office. Currently, the wives of the deceased Principal Chiefs of Phamong, Berea, Maama and 'M'amathe, for example, have succeeded their husbands and are members of the Senate. It is also common practice that senior wives of chiefs act on behalf of their minor sons until they come of age. Even prior to independence, Chieftainess 'M'antšebo Seeiso was appointed to be regent after the death of her husband, Paramount Chief Seeiso Griffith, in 1940, until the late King Moshoeshoe II took over the throne in 1960. In Lesotho, therefore, a chief is defined in terms of Order No. 26 of 1970 and the Chieftainship Act, 1968, which themselves are products of Basotho custom and tradition as embodied in the Laws of Lerotholi.

The role of traditional leadership in public life

The importance of the institution of chieftainship in the public life of the Basotho is recognised by different sectors of society, including the country's political leadership, civil society organisations, academics and elected local councillors. They regard it as an embodiment of the Basotho identity, culture and nationhood and believe that it performs many important functions, including the maintenance of law and order, registers of birth and death, livestock registers, authentication of stock and land ownership in rural areas, the maintenance of peace through conflict resolution, and various other functions. The chiefs have been given powers to regulate political rallies and demonstrations in their areas under the Public Processions Act, 2010. This function potentially gives them significant political power and influence, in that they can allow or disallow the holding of political rallies. If, for example, any political party were to hold a rally to elect candidates for parliamentary elections, a chief of the area may or may not allow such a rally. This means the fate of a powerful person like a Member of Parliament (MP) could be decided by a village chief. However, there is no evidence that chiefs have used this power to obstruct any political party or election candidate.

Systems of accountability of traditional leadership

The institution of chieftainship is formally part of government bureaucracy in Lesotho, because its administration and regulation is located in the Ministry of Local Government and Chieftainship Affairs. This makes it no different from other state agencies in terms of accountability. It falls under the direct authority of the Minister of Local Government and Chieftainship Affairs. For example, no chief can assume office without the approval of the King acting in accordance with the advice of the Minister, no authority can discipline a chief without the Minister being present and chairing such disciplinary proceedings or having appointed someone to act on behalf of such Minister, and no one other than such disciplinary committee has the power to impose on any chief such sanctions as reprimand or depriving a chief of some or all of his/her powers and duties. Since the advent of elected local councils, the chiefs no longer handle any public funds. In the past, they used to be responsible for collecting grazing fees from farmers through impounded livestock. This function has since been transferred to the elected councils. There is also a provision for senior chiefs to discipline lower chiefs. This provision allows the removal of chiefs from office in cases of extreme incompetence or ill-discipline. However, despite the presence of this mechanism, chiefs are rarely disciplined, as the processes can take a very long time. Furthermore, such chiefs usually receive lenient sentences, as, in most cases, senior chiefs and their juniors are brothers. Nevertheless, chiefs largely remain accountable and committed to serving their peoples. This is attributable to the upbringing and cultural education of the chiefs, which shape their orientation and value system and acceptance of their responsibility to authorities. They regularly consult with the people under their authority in the form of the lipitso. These lipitso consultations become possible because the chiefs reside in the same locations as their subjects, and therefore no complicated logistical preparations are needed. The chiefs can be, and indeed have been, suspended from their duties when considered by the government to have failed to carry out duties efficiently or were seen to be defying the government. Such cases include the forced exile and ultimate dethronement of the former King Moshoeshoe II by the Military Government in 1990. In response to this dethronement, Chief Khoabane Theko of Thaba-Bosiu spoke publicly against the move and was consequently suspended by the regime.

The debate on the role of traditional leadership

There has been limited debate in the literature on the role of the chieftainship in Lesotho. Based on liberal democratic theory, some authors argue for the abolition of the country's system of chieftainship. Rugege, for instance, maintains that 'hereditary rule is fundamentally undemocratic. The right to exercise power over their fellow citizens is not derived from a democratic mandate from the people but from the accident of their birth in a ruling family ... ' Besides, in his view, the chiefs abuse their power. They are corrupt and unaccountable to their people. They are only accountable to those who pay their salaries, irrespective of the nature of the regime in power. While some of Rugege's criticisms of the chiefs may be plausible, the chiefs are in fact accountable to democratically elected political leaders. Without justifying other politically immoral actions, such as abuse of power and corruption, of which Rugege accuses the chiefs, these excesses are also rampant among elected politicians. The chieftainship has in some instances in fact acted in ways that have protected citizens against the abuse of power by politicians(see case study 5).

Makoa also supports the abolition of the chieftainship in Lesotho, arguing that the conditions which gave rise to the institution no longer exist; and that it is a drain on national resources, which could be used for the provision of important public services. Consequently, he argues, it has no role in Lesotho. However, later empirical studies find that the institution of chieftainship is still extremely important in Lesotho. In a comparative, cross-national study of 14 countries in Africa, including Lesotho, Logan found that the Basotho rank number four in terms of the trust they place in the chieftainship and in the Prime Minister. They accorded similar scores of 58% to both, while the elected councils scored 49%. Similarly, Kapa also finds that the chieftainship continues to be regarded as relevant by political leaders, civil society organisations, academics, and elected councillors in Lesotho, given the ideological and practical functions it performs in Basotho society. Despite some minor differences, especially on the part of politicians, as to whether or not the chiefs should play a more active role in politics by way of running for political office, there is general consensus in society that the chieftainship remains relevant and plays an important role in the daily life of the Basotho. There is also a strong feeling that the chieftainship is neglected by the government in terms of training and that the Chieftainship Act, 1968, is outdated and in need of amendment to accommodate whatever new challenges may be confronting the chieftainship. :

Interaction of the chieftainship with elected national Parliament

In March 2008, Principal Chiefs in the upper House of Parliament voted unanimously against the sixth Constitutional Amendment Bill whose object was to enable appeal against High Court judgments on election-related disputes.

The Constitution, in section 69(6), provides that determination by the High Court on questions concerning election-related disputes shall not be subject to appeal. The ruling Lesotho Congress for Democracy (LCD) wanted the Constitution to be amended so that the case, still before the High Court, on the allocation of 40 Proportional representation (Pr) seats could be heard by the Court of Appeal. This was a highly sensitive case, with the potential of causing the ruling party to lose 21 seats, leading to a majority of only 62 seats in a 120-member National Assembly.

The argument of the chiefs in the upper House was that the bill should wait until the High Court had made its ruling so that the bill would not be construed as an attempt to pre-empt the outcome of the case. They argued that to pass the bill at that juncture would be tantamount to abuse of power by the ruling party designed to manipulate the Constitution in order to protect its government. The ruling party had secured the two-thirds majority required to pass the bill in the National Assembly, but had to secure a two-thirds majority in the senate as well, as per the requirements of the Constitution under section 85(3)(b), which is one of the entrenched clauses of the Constitution. As a result of the decision by the chiefs to vote against the bill, some government Ministers threatened the chiefs with the possibility of abolishing the senate and consequently also the chieftainship. But the chiefs vowed that they were acting in the national rather than in partisan interest and were ready to face a referendum if need be.

Conclusion and recommendations

The institution of chieftainship and individual chiefs enjoy state recognition through the national Constitution and the Chieftainship Act, 1968. However, chiefs are not appropriately remunerated by the government as is, for example, the case with councillors. The government also does not provide them with relevant training alongside councillors. Consequently, the government should urgently review salaries and allowances of chiefs in recognition of the valuable contribution they make to the Basotho nation. It should also organise appropriate training for chiefs on a regular basis to empower them to do their work even better.

Chapter Ten

Development assistance and foreign relations

This chapter attempts to establish the extent to which foreign policy and foreign relations in Lesotho are subject to the rules of democratic accountability. It therefore focuses on external assistance for the improvement of the functioning of government bodies and civil society organisations in the promotion of public consultation on matters of foreign policy. In particular, the chapter addresses the following issues: democratic debate and foreign policy, access to information, harmonisation of financial resources, conditionality, and aid in support of democratic development.

Democratic debate and foreign policy

In parliamentary systems, the executive is regarded as a committee of Parliament. This implies that the executive will have to consult the legislature regularly on matters of national importance, such as major foreign-policy issues. Heywood captures this issue well by noting that, in theory, the legislature has the upper hand over the executive, because it has the ultimate power and ability to remove the latter. In practice, however, parliamentary systems are 'often associated with the problem of executive domination', such as is the case in Britain, 'where the combination of strict party discipline and a disproportional electoral system [...] normally allows government to control parliament through a cohesive and reliable majority in the House of Commons.' In southern Africa, the process of democratisation has produced one-party-dominant systems, which have witnessed the executive branch wielding more power than other arms of the state, especially the legislature. Lesotho has not been an exception to this general situation. Under these conditions of dominance by the ruling parties – the Basutoland Congress Party (BCP) (from 1993 to 1998) and the Lesotho Congress for Democracy (LCD) (from 1998 to date) – foreign policy has always been the special province of the executive. Foreign policy and relations with development partners are not subject to democratic debate in Parliament. All negotiations and agreements between Lesotho and external financial institutions or foreign governments, and all international treaties, conventions and protocols, are concluded and signed by the executive without consulting the legislature. Civil society organisations (CSOs) attempted to lobby and influence the executive on the passing of the Land Bill, 2010, which was generally regarded by many sections of the population as being heavily influenced by the United States of America, as a precondition for Lesotho receiving a huge grant of USD362. 5 million under the United States Millennium Challenge Account. This bill had caused huge controversy across different sections of the Basotho population, including non-governmental organisations (NGOs), opposition political parties and their youth leagues, academics, as well as the chiefs, as reflected in the local media. The issues of contention about the bill were the clauses on land appropriation by the state, allowing foreign enterprises to own land in Lesotho, the nature and scope of public participation in the discussion of the bill, and the removal of the chiefs from the land-allocation process. However, all these protests failed and the bill was passed into law.

Access to information

Information on external development assistance to Lesotho is not readily accessible from any single source and can only be found in bits and pieces from various sources, rather than from, say, the annual national budget. Some of the information is contained in annual budget speeches and some in documents of development partners available on the internet. However, these are not sufficiently detailed to provide a general picture in terms of overall amounts allocated to specific sectors or of the identities of contributing agencies or development partners. An attempt is made in this report to provide information about development assistance available from different sources, but the author of the report does not claim that the information is comprehensive or even realistically reflects actual figures.

The national budget does not provide detailed information about the exact sources and value of assistance per fiscal year or per sector. The following examples regarding the last three fiscal years illustrate the point. In the 2010/2011 fiscal year, the total national budget was estimated at about M8 183. 5 million (USD1 169. 7 million), of which M1 809. 1 million (USD258. 4 million) was received from external sources in the form of grants and soft loans. This funding was to support water-supply projects, of which the construction of the Metolong Water Scheme was the main beneficiary. The funds came from the following sources: the International Development Association; the European Development Fund; Irish Aid; the Kuwait Fund for International Development; the South African government; the Millennium Challenge Account (MCA) of the United States of America; the Organisation of Petroleum Exporting Countries (OPEC); Arab Bank for Economic Development in Africa (BADEA); the Saudi Fund; and the European Investment Bank. In the 2011/2012 fiscal year, the national budget approved by Parliament was estimated at M10 244. 6 million (USD1 463. 5 million), of which M6 575. 0 million (USD939. 3 million) and M3 569. 6 million (USD509. 9) were allocated for recurrent and capital expenditure respectively. The Budget Speech reflects that the water sector was supported by the same development partners as above, to the amount of over M70 million (USD10 million). Again, there are no details on the individual contribution by each partner. Apart from the water sector, some multilateral financial institutions and Arab development partners contributed funds towards an amount of M5 444. 4 million (USD777. 8) allocated by the government of Lesotho to road construction and rehabilitation projects in many parts of the country. The specific development partners and the value of their individual contributions were again not identified.

The revenue budget of Lesotho has increased to M13. 7 billion in the 2012/2013 fiscal year, while the total expenditure is estimated at M13. 9 billion, with M8. 4 billion as recurrent expenditure and M5. 4 billion as capital expenditure. Development partners again contributed to the water sector to a combined value of M1. 6 billion to finance the Metolong Water Scheme, with such development partners being: the European Investment Bank; the South African government; BADEA; OPEC; the Kuwait Fund; the MCA; Abu Dhabi; and the Saudi Fund. Again, the individual contribution of each partner is not indicated. Village and rural water-supply programmes are to be supported by funds from Irish Aid, the European Development Fund, the World Bank and the MCA to an amount of M50 million, also without a clear indication as to how much each financier will contribute. Other than this general information, the Budget Speech does not provide any further useful data.

The Southern African Customs Union (SACU) has been the main provider of financial resources for Lesotho, averaging 54.5% of its total revenue between 1981 and 2009. The SACU collects duties on local production, and customs duties on its members' imports from outside the customs area, and the revenue collected is allocated to its member states (South Africa, Botswana, Lesotho, Swaziland and Namibia) in quarterly instalments based on an agreed revenue-sharing formula. In recent years, however, the SACU revenues have been declining significantly to the extent that, in the 2010/2011 financial year, the receipts from this source had declined by 53.43% from M4 918.00 million to M2 627.90 million.

Harmonisation of financial resources

The external financial resources of the country are, to a large extent, coordinated and integrated into the national policy planning and accountability systems. This is in line with the Paris Declaration on Aid Effectiveness. This was noted by the

Minister of Finance and Development Planning when he expressed the following sentiments:

Though there are many donors, [...], the amazing thing is the level of coordination and cooperation among them. This has made our work easier. I thank them for [...] their success in implanting the Paris Principles of Government ownership of development programmes; aligning of Donor policies behind government policies and procedures and coordination among Donors and Government. In addition to the coordination of external assistance efforts, the Ministry of Finance and Development Planning has established within itself a special unit (the AID Coordination Unit) to coordinate all aid resources and to integrate them into the national budget. Development partners provide finance by sector, project and general budget support, although there is a general move towards general budget support. While in the last few years project funding was common, this was found to be costly, as some of the money was used to pay for other costs of a recurrent nature, thus leaving a reduced amount for capital projects. The approach now is towards sector budgeting and general budget support where development partners sit together with government officials and discuss and agree on areas needing support. The existing national systems and structures are used and this helps cut costs which would otherwise be incurred. Continuity of international development assistance funds on a multiyear basis depends on the results and performance of the government in relation to previous resources provided. Each programme has its own built-in evaluation mechanisms to determine how well or effectively resources have been used. Funds provided by development partners may therefore be increased or decreased, depending on the performance of the government based on the initial agreement between government and development partners. These funds are also subject to national systems of accountability; they are presented to Parliament as a total national budget and are subjected to normal auditing processes carried out by the Auditor General. External funds are in some cases tied to the use of particular suppliers or consultants. But, in most cases, the government is free to use suppliers and consultants of its own choosing. 280 Bilateral and multilateral development partners harmonise their activities around national

policy documents reflective of broad consultations with government ministries, and provide assistance on the basis of these. 281 The key national policy documents in this regard are the National Vision 2020 (a paper that was developed during a broadly consultative process involving broad representation of several sections of the population), the Poverty Reduction

Strategy Paper (PRSP) and the new Five Year National Strategic Development Plan, which seeks to implement the Vision 2020.

Conditionality

Donors' conditionality is no longer a big issue for development partners. Conditionality in this context means the link between the approval or continuation of funding by one country or agency and the implementation of specific elements of economic policy by a country receiving such assistance. They allow flexibility in the use of the resources they provide, although the government has to use the money for the purpose it was allocated for. The purpose of periodic evaluation by the government and development partners is to determine that resources are used as intended, and it is on this basis that assistance may be increased, decreased or terminated. As such, there are no stringent conditions imposed by development partners that would hinder democratic development. Rather, they provide assistance in ways that promote democratic development. However, the promulgation of the Land Act, 2010, provoked intense national debate, as shown elsewhere in this report. The ruling party's election manifesto did not include any reference to this act, and it was hastily introduced by government. This example could be regarded as an externally imposed policy that the executive had no option but to implement in order to receive financial assistance from the United States government.

Aid supporting democratic development

Lesotho has, in the post-1993 period, established some democracy-protection institutions which receive funding from development partners. These include the Office of the Ombudsman, the Directorate on Corruption and Economic Offences (DCEO) and the Independent Electoral Commission (IEC). The United Nations Development Programme (UNDP) under its fourth United Nations Development Assistance Framework (UNDAF) also plays a huge role in supporting democracy-promotion institutions, in Lesotho in line with the country's Vision 2020. The UNDAF document states that 'the expectation is that by 2020, governance institutions are strengthened, thereby ensuring gender equity, improved public service delivery and human rights for all'. In this connection, the UNDAF 'will seek to ensure strengthened governance institutions for a stable participatory democracy and effective economic oversight'. In this regard, the whole United Nations system, in collaboration with other development partners, including Irish Aid and the European Union (EU), provide assistance under three programmes, the following of which are relevant to this report. Firstly, the Consolidating Democracy and

Good Governance (CDGG) programme, a five-year programme (2008–2012) with a budget of USD3 million, provides support in three areas: harmonisation and streamlining of electoral legislation to ensure that elections add value to democracy, governance and political stability; parliamentary reforms to improve the effectiveness of law-making, representation and the oversight functions of Parliament; and the promotion and protection of human rights. The UNDP and Irish Aid work in partnership with the IEC, Parliament and the Ministry of Justice, Human Rights and Correctional Service, and the Office of the Ombudsman. Secondly, the two partners have also supported the government through the Lesotho Local Development Programme. This programme focuses on institutional development and capacity-building, in respect of aspects of decentralisation and local development, through the development of systems and procedures for community service infrastructure and service delivery. The third programme, Collaborative Capacities Enhancement, provides support in the establishment of an election-related, conflict-resolution mechanism. It funded the efforts of the Christian Council of Lesotho (a body made up of different Christian church denominations) to resolve the post-2007 election conflict regarding the allocation of Proportional Representation (PR) seats between the opposition parties and the ruling party. The programme also focuses on reviewing past and existing conflict-resolution mechanisms to determine how they can be strengthened to prevent future conflicts related to elections, including the 2012 elections. In this regard, these development partners work closely with key political actors, such as the leadership of political parties, staff of the IEC, leaders of churches, chiefs and the Ombudsman. The programme also sponsors training of these actors.

Assistance to civil society organisations for engagement with government bodies

The UNDAF also commits itself to strengthening the capacity of CSOs to function as effective watchdogs 'to ensure a stable, participatory democracy and equitable government spending in support of economic growth'. In this regard, the UNDP supported one local CSO, the Transformation Resource Centre (TRC), in its efforts to engage with political parties, the youth and the media to accelerate progress towards achievement of the Millennium Development Goals (MDGs). This programme sought to mobilise these groups to play their different roles

towards the attainment of the MDGs. Political parties were expected to commit themselves to the MDGs and to include them in their election manifestos and campaign programmes. The media had to contribute by playing an advocacy role with regard to the MDGs, while the youth were expected to voice their concerns and influence policy towards addressing those concerns. The programme was thus intended to build the capacity of these groups to play these roles. 292 The UNDP has also donated vehicles to, and sponsored capacity-building workshops for, the staff of the Lesotho Council of Non-Governmental Organisations (LCN). It will hopefully also engage in more projects with civil society under the next UNDAF in order to build more capacity to ensure effectiveness in the deepening of democracy.

Conclusion and recommendations

The legislative arm of the state in Lesotho is weak in relation to the executive. The latter makes important decisions regarding foreign-policy issues, including the signing of international treaties, without these being subject to democratic debate in the legislature. Access to information relating to development assistance is scant and scattered and not easily accessible from a single point of reference. Information has to be distilled from annual budget speeches made by the Minister of Finance to Parliament (available on the government website) and can also partly be accessed from the donor community, such as the UNDP, through its website. Complete and detailed information, however, is not available. Financial resources are harmonised and coordinated in keeping with the Paris Declaration on Aid Effectiveness. Development partners generally do not impose conditionalities on the assistance they provide. They work closely with the government under mutually agreed terms based on how funds have been used by the government in previous years. Several development partners, under the umbrella of the UNDP, provide aid in support of democratic development. The main beneficiaries of such assistance, which was intended largely for capacity-building, have been the IEC, DCEO, the Office of Ombudsman, Parliament and the Ministry of Justice. The UNDP has also provided assistance for the TRC to enable it to engage with the media, the youth and political parties concerning projects that contribute to the achievement of the MDGs.

Given that issues of foreign policy and international agreements have profound and long- term effects on a nation, it is crucial for these policies to be subjected to democratic debate. The government should therefore consult Parliament before it signs international treaties and agreements so that these first obtain the blessing of the representatives of the people and, in this way, become legitimate policy.

www.ingramcontent.com/pod-product-compliance
Lightning Source LLC
Chambersburg PA
CBHW031106080526
44587CB00011B/852